cook's library

Wok &
Stir-Fry

cook's library

Wok & Stir-Fry

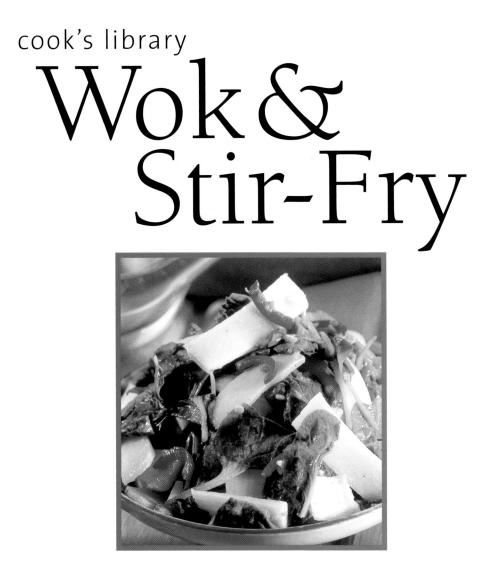

This is a Parragon Publishing Book
This edition published in 2004

Parragon Publishing
Queen Street House
4 Queen Street
Bath BA1 1HE, UK

ISBN: 0-75259-957-7

Printed in China

NOTE

Cup measurements in this book are for American cups. This book
uses imperial and metric measurements. Follow the same units of
measurement throughout; do not mix imperial and metric. All spoon
measurements are level: teaspoons are assumed to be 5 ml,
and tablespoons are assumed to be 15 ml. Unless otherwise stated,
milk is assumed to be full fat, eggs and individual vegetables such
as potatoes are medium, and pepper is freshly ground black pepper.

The times given for each recipe are an approximate guide only because
the preparation times may differ according to the techniques used by
different people and the cooking times may vary as a result of the type
of oven used. The preparation times include chilling and marinating
times, where appropriate.

Recipes using raw or very lightly cooked eggs should be avoided
by infants, the elderly, pregnant women, convalescents, and anyone
suffering from an illness.

Contents

Introduction

One of the quickest, easiest, and most versatile methods of cooking is to cook in a wok. It takes only a few minutes to assemble the ingredients—a selection of vegetables, to which may be added meat, fish, seafood, bean curd, nuts, rice, or noodles. The possibilities are endless for ringing the changes with different oils, seasonings, and sauces, and the result is a colorful, delicious, healthy meal that is as pleasing to the eye as it is to the taste buds.

Wok

A wok is a metal cooking implement in the shape of a shallow, curved bowl, with either one long wooden handle or two looped handles. The wok comes in a variety of sizes—one approximately 12–14-inches/30–35-cm in diameter is suitable for the average family—and, as with most kitchen equipment, it is worth investing in the best you can afford. Woks are made from stainless steel, copper, or cast iron, and the latter is ideal as it retains heat more efficiently, especially once it has become well-seasoned.

Although it is possible to cook in a skillet, there are several good reasons to use a wok. The key to successful cooking is to move and toss the ingredients constantly as they go in, and this is much easier to achieve in the convex shape of a wok. The curved sides allow the heat to rise, so that the whole wok becomes hot, speeding up the cooking process; and as the food cannot become lodged in corners or edges, it is extremely easy to clean the wok after use.

Wok Seasoning and Cleaning

New woks, apart from those with a non-stick lining, must be seasoned before they are used. First wash well with hot water and cream cleanser to remove the protective coating of oil. Rinse and dry the wok and then place it over a low heat and add about 2 tablespoons of vegetable oil. Rub the oil all over the inner surface of the wok with a thick pad of paper towel, taking care not to burn your fingers. Heat the oil for about 10 minutes, then wipe it off with a fresh pad of paper towel, which will become black. Repeat this heating and wiping process until the paper towel remains clean; it will take quite a long time.

Once the wok has been seasoned, it should not be washed with cream cleanser or detergent. Simply wipe it out with paper towel, wash in hot water and dry thoroughly. If the wok is used only occasionally, it may become rusty. In this case, scour the rust off and season again.

Wok Accessories

Some woks are supplied with lids, but if not, these can be bought separately. They are dome-shaped, usually made of aluminum and are tight-fitting. A lid is necessary when the wok is used for steaming, but a dome-shaped pan lid will work as satisfactorily.

A metal stand is an essential safety feature when the wok is used for steaming, braising, or deep-frying. It may be an open-sided frame or a perforated metal ring.

A wok scoop is a bowl-shaped spatula with a long handle. Some resemble a perforated spoon and others are made from reinforced wire mesh. The handle may be wood or metal. The scoop makes it easier to toss the ingredients during stir-frying, but a long-handled spoon is an adequate substitute. Chinese cooks also use the scoop for adding ingredients to the wok.

A trivet is used for steaming. It is placed in the base of the wok and supports the dish or plate containing the food above the water level. It may be made of wood or metal.

A wok brush of split bamboo is used for cleaning the wok.

For steaming bamboo baskets with lids are available in a range of sizes and can be stacked one on top of another. They are designed to rest on the sloping sides of the wok above the water level.

The cleaver is a finely balanced tool and is seen in every Chinese kitchen. It is used for virtually all cutting tasks, from chopping spare ribs and halving duck to slashing fish and deveining shrimps. Cleavers are available in a variety of weights and sizes and although they look unwieldy, they are precision instruments. The blade should be kept razor sharp.

Long wooden chopsticks may be used for adding ingredients to the wok, fluffing rice, separating noodles and general stirring. They are not essential, but are useful and add a feeling of authenticity. Because they have a lighter touch than a spoon or fork, they are less likely to break up or squash delicate ingredients. Chopsticks are easy to handle once you have acquired the knack. Place one chopstick in the angle between your thumb and index finger, with the lower part resting on your middle finger. Hold the other chopstick between the thumb and index finger as you would hold a pencil; this is the one you manipulate.

Regional Cooking

Although its popularity is now far more wide-ranging, wok cooking originated in Asia and the Far East, where variations of this useful implement are commonly used in the preparation of many dishes. In India, the curry derives its name from karahi, a large pan that sits over a hole in a brick or earth stove and is used for braising and cooking, while in Mongolia the convex iron griddle used for charbroiling meat, especially lamb, is very similar in shape to a wok.

It was the Chinese, however, who devised cooking in a wok. There are regional variations in ingredients throughout this vast country, but fresh vegetables play a very important role in all Chinese cooking. This rapid and efficient method of cooking the vegetables ensures that they retain their individual flavors, their vibrant colors, and their crisp texture, as well as preserving their vitamin content. Poultry, lamb, beef, and pork are also cooked in the wok — either deep-fried or steamed—and are combined with sauces and seasonings. Long- or short-grain white rice is often added or served as an accompaniment, and noodles made from wheat, buckwheat, or rice flours are also widely used.

Chinese influence has spread to its neighboring countries as well. Throughout Indonesia, Japan, Thailand, Singapore, and Malaysia, the wok is used over wood or charcoal for curries and rice dishes as well as stir-fries, with variations in the addition of different meat, fish, vegetables, spices, and sauces.

A style of cuisine that has enjoyed a huge rise in popularity in recent years is Thai. For the people of Thailand, the preparation and eating of good food, beautifully served, is taken very seriously. The ingredients, locally grown and used very fresh, are carefully chosen and skillfully balanced for texture and flavor, combining bitter, salt, sour, hot, and sweet tastes.

Thai cuisine lends itself perfectly to stir-frying. There are many Thai foods that are cooked in a wok, either one-pot noodle dishes or soups, or vegetable, meat, or fish side dishes.

The monsoon climate and abundant rainfall in Thailand produce ideal conditions for growing rice, so it's not surprising that Thai cuisine is centered around this, the country's most important staple. Thai fragrant rice is a long-grain, fluffy white rice, delicately scented, while glutinous rice is short-grain with a high starch content, which makes it sticky when cooked. Rice flour is also used to make noodles, usually in the shape of flat ribbons or thin vermicelli.

The warm Gulf seas around Thailand, and the inland waterways, produce a wide variety of fish in abundance, and in all the coastal towns fresh seafood is sold from thatch-roofed beach kiosks—charbroiled or sautéed fish with ginger, shrimp with coconut milk and cilantro, or steamed crab. Meat is often combined with seafood, such as shrimp or crab meat.

Other essentials in Thai cooking are coconut (almost as important as rice), lime, chile, garlic, lemongrass, gingerroot, and cilantro, as well as seasonings, such as soy sauce, rice vinegar, and fish sauce. All of these ingredients are now readily available in your local food store.

Cooking Techniques

Although the wok can be used for steaming and deep-frying, its main use is for stir-frying. In China, where this is the most widely used method of cooking, it is called *Ch'au*, a term that describes cooking a number of ingredients, thinly sliced, in oil. As it cooks, the food is tossed and turned with long bamboo chopsticks.

There are two basic types of cooking, known as *Pao* and *Liu*. *Pao*, or "explosion", is a method where the food is stirred rapidly in a dry wok over the highest heat for about one minute. Foods cooked in this way are often marinated beforehand for flavor and tenderness. *Liu* is wet frying, where the foods are constantly turned until cooked. Peanut or corn oil are usually used for such cooking. Sesame oil burns easily, but can be drizzled over the finished dish as a seasoning.

Some foods need a slightly longer cooking time than others and, for this reason, cooking is often done in stages. This also allows the individual ingredients to retain their distinct flavors. As they cook, the foods are removed from the wok, but they are always combined once everything is cooked, and served as a whole dish. In *Liu*, a mixture of cornstarch and bouillon is added to the wok at the end of cooking, together with sugar, vinegar, and soy sauce, to make a delicious, almost sticky, coating sauce.

There is plenty of scope for creativity when choosing ingredients, even for the simplest stir-fry. A combination of onions, carrots, bell peppers (green, red, yellow, and orange), broccoli, and snow peas will provide the basis for a colorful dish. Add beansprouts at the end of cooking and toss quickly for texture, or some canned water chestnuts, which add a delicious crunch. A few cashews or almonds, some cubed bean curd or chicken breast, or a handful of shrimp provide protein, while adding some pre-cooked rice or noodles makes a gutsy stir-fry. A ready-made sauce—perhaps oyster, or yellow bean—will finish off the dish. Ginger, garlic, and chiles are wonderful for flavoring stir-fries. Chiles come in a wide variety, ranging in heat from very mild to fiery hot. Red chiles are slightly sweeter and hotter than green, and larger chiles also tend to be milder. Crushed dried chilis are useful for seasoning. The Thais favor the small red or green "bird's-eye" chiles, which are very fiery, and their curries are flavored with ferociously hot chili pastes.

Some of the "kick" can be taken out of a hot chile by removing the seeds, but this must be done very carefully as they can cause a nasty reaction if contact is made with the skin. Cut fresh chiles in half, and scrape out the seeds with the point of a knife, and with dried chilis, simply cut off the end and shake out the seeds. Always remember to wash your hands afterwards!

How to Use This Book

Each recipe contains a wealth of useful information, including a breakdown
of nutritional quantities, preparation and cooking times, and level of difficulty.
All of this information is explained in detail below.

A full-color photograph
of the finished dish.

The ingredients for
each recipe are listed
in the order that they
are used.

The nutritional
information provided
for each recipe is per
serving or per portion.
Optional ingredients,
variations or serving
suggestions have not
been included in the
calculations.

The method is clearly
explained with step-by-
step instructions that
are easy to follow.

Cook's tips provide useful
information regarding
ingredients or cooking
techniques.

17

WOK & STIR-FRY

The green lentils used in
this recipe require soaking
but it is worth the time for
the flavor. If time is short,
use red lentils, which do
not require soaking.

Green Lentil Pan-Fry

SERVES 4

3¼ cups dried green lentils
4 tbsp butter or vegetarian margarine
2 garlic cloves, crushed
2 tbsp olive oil
1 tbsp cider vinegar
1 red onion, cut into 8 pieces
1¾ oz/50 g baby corn cobs,
 halved lengthwise
1 yellow bell pepper, seeded and
 cut into strips
1 red bell pepper, seeded and cut
 into strips
1¾ oz/50 g green beans, halved
½ cup vegetable bouillon
2 tbsp honey
salt and pepper
crusty bread, to serve

1 Soak the lentils in a large pan of cold water for 25 minutes. Bring to the boil,
 reduce the heat and simmer for 20 minutes. Drain thoroughly.

2 Add 1 tablespoon of the butter, 1 garlic clove, 1 tablespoon of oil, and the
 cider vinegar to the lentils and mix well.

3 Melt the remaining butter, garlic, and oil in a preheated wok or large, heavy-
 based skillet and cook the onion, baby corn cobs, yellow and red bell peppers,
 and beans for 3–4 minutes.

4 Add the vegetable bouillon and bring to a boil. Cook the mixture for about
 10 minutes, or until the liquid has evaporated.

5 Add the honey and season with salt and pepper to taste. Stir in the lentil
 mixture and cook for 1 minute to heat through. Spoon on to warmed serving
 plates and serve with crusty bread.

NUTRITION
Calories 490; Sugars 12 g; Protein 26 g;
Carbohydrates 61 g; Fat 18 g; Saturates 8 g

easy
30 mins
45 mins

COOK'S TIP

This stir-fry is very versatile—you can use a mixture of your favorite vegetables,
if you prefer, such as zucchini, carrots, or snow peas.

The number of stars represents the
difficulty of each recipe, ranging from
very easy (1 star) to challenging (4 stars).

This amount of time represents the
preparation of ingredients, including
cooling, chilling and soaking times.

This represents the cooking time.

Soups *and* Appetizers

Soup is indispensable at Asian tables, especially in China, Japan, Korea, and South-East Asia. It is generally eaten part way through a main meal to clear the palate for further dishes. There are many different types of delicious soups, both thick and thin and, of course, the clear soups which are often served with wontons or dumplings.

Appetizers or snacks are drier foods in general; the spring roll is a well-known Chinese snack and these come in many variations and shapes across the Far East. Other delights are wrapped in pastry, bread, and rice paper or are skewered for ease of eating; vegetables, fish, and meat are also deep-fried for a crispy coating. These dishes are served as appetizers in Westernized restaurants to animate the tastebuds in anticipation of the main course.

Hot and sour soups are found across South-East Asia in different forms. Reduce the number of chiles added if you prefer a milder dish.

Hot *and* Sour Mushroom Soup

SERVES 4

2 tbsp tamarind paste
4 fresh red chiles, chopped very finely
2 garlic cloves, crushed
2 tsp finely chopped fresh gingerroot
4 tbsp fish sauce
2 tbsp palm sugar or superfine sugar
8 lime leaves, torn roughly
5 cups vegetable bouillon
1 large carrot, sliced thinly
8 oz/225 g white mushrooms, halved
12 oz/350 g white cabbage, shredded
3½ oz/100 g fine green beans, halved
3 tbsp coarsely chopped fresh cilantro
3½ oz/100 g cherry tomatoes, halved

1 Place the tamarind paste, chiles, garlic, ginger, fish sauce, palm sugar, lime leaves, and vegetable bouillon in a large preheated wok or large, heavy-based pan. Bring the mixture to the boil, stirring occasionally.

2 Reduce the heat and add the carrots, mushrooms, white cabbage, and green beans. Leave the soup to simmer, uncovered, for about 10 minutes, or until the vegetables are tender, but not soft.

3 Stir the fresh cilantro and cherry tomatoes into the mixture in the wok and heat through for another 5 minutes.

4 Transfer the soup to a warm soup tureen or individual serving bowls and serve immediately.

NUTRITION
Calories *87*; Sugars *7 g*; Protein *4 g*;
Carbohydrate *8 g*; Fat *5 g*; Saturates *1 g*

easy

10 mins

20 mins

🍳 COOK'S TIP

Tamarind is the dried fruit of the tamarind tree. Sold as a pulp or paste, it is used to give a special sweet and sour flavor to Asian dishes.

Crab and corn are classic ingredients in Chinese cooking. Here, egg noodles are added for a filling dish.

Crab *and* Sweetcorn Soup

1 Heat the sunflower oil in a preheated wok or large, heavy-based pan.

2 Add the Chinese five-spice powder, carrots, corn, peas, scallions, and chile to the wok and cook for about 5 minutes, stirring constantly.

3 Add the crab meat to the wok and cook the mixture for 1 minute, distributing the crab meat evenly.

4 Roughly break up the egg noodles and add to the wok.

5 Pour the fish bouillon and soy sauce into the mixture in the wok and bring to a boil.

6 Cover the wok and let the soup simmer for 5 minutes.

7 Stir once more, then transfer the soup to a warm soup tureen or individual serving bowls and serve at once.

SERVES 4

1 tbsp sunflower oil
1 tsp Chinese five-spice powder
3 small carrots, cut into sticks
1/2 cup canned or frozen corn kernels
3/4 cup frozen peas
6 scallions, trimmed and sliced
1 fresh red chile, seeded and very
   thinly sliced
14 oz/400 g can white crab meat
6 oz/175 g egg noodles
7 1/2 cups fish bouillon
3 tbsp soy sauce

NUTRITION
Calories *324*; Sugars *6 g*; Protein *27 g*;
Carbohydrate *39 g*; Fat *8 g*; Saturates *2 g*

⭐⭐   easy

🕐   5 mins

🕐   20 mins

COOK'S TIP

Chinese five-spice powder is a mixture of star anise, fennel, cloves, cinnamon, and Szechuan pepper. It has an unmistakable flavor. Use it sparingly, as it is very pungent.

Aromatic lime leaves are used as a flavoring in this soup to add tartness.

Spicy Shrimp Soup

SERVES 4

2 tbsp tamarind paste
4 fresh red chiles, chopped very finely
2 garlic cloves, crushed
2 tsp finely chopped fresh gingerroot
4 tbsp fish sauce
2 tbsp palm sugar or superfine sugar
5 cups fish bouillon
8 lime leaves, torn roughly
1 large carrot, sliced very thinly
2 cups diced sweet potatoes
3½ oz/100 g baby corn cobs, halved
3 tbsp coarsely chopped fresh cilantro
3½ oz/100 g cherry tomatoes, halved
8 oz/225 g raw fan-tail shrimp

1 Place the tamarind paste, red chiles, garlic, ginger, fish sauce, sugar, and fish bouillon in a preheated wok or large, heavy-based pan. Add the lime leaves to the wok. Bring to a boil, stirring constantly to blend the flavours.

2 Reduce the heat and add the carrot, sweet potato, and baby corn cobs to the mixture in the wok.

3 Let the soup simmer, uncovered, for about 10 minutes, or until the vegetables are just tender.

4 Stir the cilantro, cherry tomatoes, and shrimp into the soup and heat through for 5 minutes, until the shrimp have changed color.

5 Transfer to a warm soup tureen or individual serving bowls and serve hot.

NUTRITION

Calories *217*; Sugars *16 g*; Protein *16 g*;
Carbohydrate *31 g*; Fat *4 g*; Saturates *1 g*

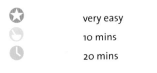

very easy

10 mins

20 mins

🍳 **COOK'S TIP**

Thai ginger or galangal is a member of the ginger family, but it is yellow in color with pink sprouts. The flavor is aromatic and less pungent than ginger.

Thai red curry paste is quite fiery, but adds a superb flavor to this dish. It is available from most large food stores.

Coconut *and* Crab Soup

1 Heat the oil in a preheated wok or large, heavy-based pan.

2 Add the red curry paste and red bell pepper to the wok and cook for 1 minute.

3 Add the coconut milk, fish bouillon, and fish sauce and bring to a boil.

4 Add the crab meat, crab claws, cilantro, and scallions to the wok.

5 Stir the mixture well and heat thoroughly for 2–3 minutes, or until everything is warmed through.

6 Transfer to a warm soup tureen or individual serving bowls and serve hot.

SERVES 4

1 tbsp peanut oil
2 tbsp red curry paste
1 red bell pepper, seeded and sliced
2$\frac{1}{2}$ cups coconut milk
2$\frac{1}{2}$ cups fish bouillon
2 tbsp fish sauce
8 oz/225 g canned or fresh white crab meat
8 oz/225 g fresh or frozen crab claws
2 tbsp chopped fresh cilantro
3 scallions, sliced

NUTRITION
Calories *122*; Sugar *9 g*; Protein *11 g*
Carbohydrates *11 g*; Fat *4 g*; Saturates *1 g*

⭐⭐⭐   moderate
🕐   5 mins
🕐   10 mins

🍳 **COOK'S TIP**

Clean the wok by washing it with water, using a mild detergent if necessary, and a soft cloth or brush. Do not scrub or use any abrasive cleaners as this will scratch the surface. Dry thoroughly, then wipe the surface with a little oil.

Chinese mushrooms add an intense flavor to this soup. If they are unavailable, use open-cap mushrooms instead.

Chili Fish Soup

SERVES 4

½ oz/15 g dried Chinese mushrooms
2 tbsp sunflower oil
1 onion, sliced
1½ cups snow peas
3½ oz/100 g canned, drained
    bamboo shoots
3 tbsp sweet chili sauce
5 cups fish or vegetable bouillon
3 tbsp light soy sauce
2 tbsp fresh cilantro, plus extra to
    garnish (optional)
1 lb/450 g cod fillet, skinned and cubed

1 Place the mushrooms in a large bowl. Pour enough boiling water over to cover and let stand for 5 minutes. Drain the mushrooms thoroughly in a strainer. Using a sharp knife, roughly chop the mushrooms.

2 Heat the sunflower oil in a preheated wok or large, heavy-based pan. Add the onion to the wok and cook for 5 minutes, or until softened.

3 Add the snow peas, bamboo shoots, chili sauce, bouillon, and soy sauce to the wok and bring to a boil.

4 Reduce the heat, add the cilantro and cod and let simmer for 5 minutes, or until the fish is cooked through.

5 Transfer to a warm soup tureen or individual serving bowls, garnish with extra cilantro, if liked, and serve hot.

NUTRITION
Calories *166*; Sugars *1 g*; Protein *23 g*;
Carbohydrate *4 g*; Fat *7 g*; Saturates *1 g*

⭐ very easy
🕐 15 mins
🕐 15 mins

👨‍🍳 **COOK'S TIP**

There are many different varieties of dried mushrooms, but shiitake are best in this recipe. They are not cheap, but a small amount will go a long way.

This soup is an interesting mix of colors and textures. The egg may be made into a flat omelet and added as thin strips, if preferred.

Shrimp Soup

1 Heat the oil in a preheated wok or large, heavy-based pan, swirling it around until really hot. Add the scallions and cook for 1 minute, then add the carrot and mushrooms and continue to cook for about 2 minutes.

2 Add the bouillon and bring to a boil, then season to taste with salt and pepper, Chinese five-spice powder, and soy sauce. Reduce the heat and simmer for 5 minutes.

3 If the shrimp are really large, cut them in half (reserving 4 whole shrimp, to garnish) before adding to the wok. Simmer for 3–4 minutes, until they change color.

4 Add the arugula leaves to the wok and mix well, then slowly pour in the beaten egg in a circular movement so that it cooks in threads in the soup. Adjust the seasoning and serve each portion topped with a whole shrimp.

SERVES 4

2 tbsp sunflower oil
2 scallions, sliced thinly diagonally
1 carrot, grated coarsely
4½ oz/125 g large closed-cup mushrooms, sliced thinly
4 cups fish or vegetable bouillon
½ tsp Chinese five-spice powder
1 tbsp light soy sauce
4½ oz/125 g large peeled, raw shrimp or peeled jumbo shrimp, thawed if frozen
½ bunch arugula leaves, chopped coarsely
1 egg, well beaten
salt and pepper

NUTRITION

Calories *123*; Sugars *0.2 g*; Protein *13 g*; Carbohydrate *1 g*; Fat *8 g*; Saturates *1 g*

easy

5 mins

20 mins

🍲 **COOK'S TIP**

Large open mushrooms with black gills give the best flavor but they tend to spoil the color of the soup, making it very dark. Oyster mushrooms are another alternative.

Quick to make, this hot and spicy soup is hearty and warming. If you like your food really fiery, add a chopped dried chili, or a fresh chile with its seeds.

Chicken Noodle Soup

SERVES 4

1 sheet of dried egg noodles from a 9 oz/250 g pack
1 tbsp sunflower oil
4 skinless, boneless chicken thighs, diced
1 bunch scallions, sliced
2 garlic cloves, chopped
2 tsp finely chopped fresh gingerroot
3½ cups chicken bouillon
scant 1 cup coconut milk
3 tsp red curry paste
3 tbsp peanut butter
2 tbsp light soy sauce
1 small red bell pepper, chopped
½ cup frozen peas
salt and pepper

NUTRITION

Calories *140*; Sugars *3 g*; Protein *3 g*;
Carbohydrate *20 g*; Fat *17 g*; Saturates *1 g*

easy

15 mins

25 mins

1 Put the noodles in a shallow dish and pour over enough boiling water to cover. Let stand as instructed on the package.

2 Heat the oil in a preheated wok or large, heavy-based pan.

3 Add the chicken to the wok and cook for 5 minutes, stirring constantly until lightly browned.

4 Add the white part of the scallions, reserving the green tops, garlic, and ginger, and cook for 2 minutes, stirring.

5 Stir in the chicken bouillon, coconut milk, red curry paste, peanut butter, and soy sauce, then bring to a boil.

6 Season with salt and pepper to taste. Reduce the heat, stirring, then simmer for 8 minutes, stirring occasionally.

7 Add the red bell pepper, peas, and green scallion tops and cook for another 2 minutes.

8 Add the drained noodles and heat through. Spoon into a warm soup tureen or individual serving bowls and serve with a spoon and fork.

COOK'S TIP

Thai green curry paste can be used instead of Thai red curry paste for a less fiery flavor.

Cornmeal can be found in most food stores or health food stores. Yellow in color, it acts as a binding agent in this recipe.

Spicy Corn Fritters

1 Place the corn, chiles, garlic, lime leaves, cilantro, egg, and cornmeal in a large mixing bowl, and stir to combine.

2 Add the green beans to the ingredients in the bowl and mix well, using a wooden spoon.

3 Divide the mixture into small, evenly sized balls. Flatten the balls of mixture between the palms of your hands to form rounds.

4 Heat a little peanut oil in a preheated wok or large, heavy-based skillet until really hot. Cook the fritters, in batches, until brown and crispy on the outside, turning occasionally.

5 Let the fritters drain on paper towels while cooking the remaining fritters.

6 Transfer the fritters to warm serving plates and serve immediately.

SERVES 4

^{3}/$_4$ cup canned or frozen corn kernels
2 fresh red chiles, seeded and chopped very finely
2 garlic cloves, crushed
10 lime leaves, chopped finely
2 tbsp chopped fresh cilantro
1 large egg
^{1}/$_2$ cup cornmeal
3^1/$_2$ oz/100 g fine green beans, sliced finely
peanut oil, for frying

NUTRITION
Calories *213*; Sugars *6 g*; Protein *5 g*;
Carbohydrate *30 g*; Fat *8 g*; Saturates *1 g*

⭐⭐ easy
🕐 5 mins
🕐 15 mins

🍳 **COOK'S TIP**

Kaffir lime leaves are dark green, glossy leaves that have a lemony-lime flavor. They can be bought, either fresh or dried, from specialist Asian stores. Fresh leaves impart the most delicious flavor.

This is a really simple dish, which is perfect served with a hot chile dip.

Seven-Spice Eggplants

SERVES 4

1 lb/450 g eggplants, sliced thinly
1 egg white
3½ tbsp cornstarch
1 tsp salt
1 tbsp Chinese seven-spice powder
oil, for deep-frying

1 Place the eggplants in a strainer, sprinkle with salt, and let stand for 30 minutes. (This will remove all the bitter juices.)

2 Rinse the eggplants thoroughly and pat dry with paper towels.

3 Place the egg white in a small bowl and whip until light and foamy.

4 Using a spoon, mix together the cornstarch, salt, and Chinese seven-spice powder on a large plate.

5 Heat the oil for deep-frying in a preheated wok or large, heavy-based skillet.

6 Dip the eggplants into the egg white, and then into the cornstarch and seven-spice mixture to coat evenly.

7 Deep-fry the coated eggplant slices, in batches, for 5 minutes, or until pale golden and crispy.

8 Transfer the eggplants to paper towels and let drain. Transfer to serving plates and serve hot.

NUTRITION

Calories *169*; Sugars *2 g*; Protein *2 g*;
Carbohydrate *15 g*; Fat *12 g*; Saturates *1 g*

very easy
35 mins
20 mins

COOK'S TIP

The best oil to use for deep-frying is peanut oil, which has a high smoke point and mild flavor, so it will neither burn nor taint the food. About 2½ cups of oil is sufficient for this recipe.

This is a very sociable dish if put in the center of the table where people can help themselves, picking up pieces of bean curd with cocktail sticks.

Bean Curd *with* Peanut Sauce

1 Combine the rice wine vinegar, sugar, and salt in a pan, then bring to a boil. Reduce the heat and simmer for 2 minutes.

2 Remove the sauce from the heat and add the peanut butter, chili flakes, and barbecue sauce, stirring well until thoroughly blended.

3 To make the batter, sift the all-purpose flour into a bowl, make a well in the center and add the eggs. Draw in the flour, adding the milk slowly. Stir in the baking powder and chili powder.

4 Heat both the sunflower oil and sesame oil in a large wok or deep-fryer until a light haze appears on top.

5 Dip the bean curd triangles into the batter, then deep-fry until golden brown. (You may need to do this in batches.) Drain on paper towels.

6 Transfer the bean curd to a serving dish and serve with the peanut sauce.

SERVES 4

2 tbsp each of rice wine vinegar and sugar
1 tsp salt
3 tbsp smooth peanut butter
1/2 tsp dried chili flakes
3 tbsp barbecue sauce
4 cups sunflower oil
2 tbsp sesame oil
1 lb 2 oz/500 g marinated or plain, firm bean curd, cut into 1-inch/2.5-cm triangles

batter
4 tbsp all-purpose flour
2 eggs, beaten
4 tbsp milk
1/2 tsp baking powder
1/2 tsp chili powder

NUTRITION

Calories *140*; Sugars *3 g*; Protein *3 g*; Carbohydrate *20 g*; Fat *17 g*; Saturates *1 g*

⭐⭐⭐   moderate
🕐   15 mins
🕐   20 mins

👨‍🍳 COOK'S TIP

Bean curd is made from processed soybeans. It is white, with a soft cheese-like texture and is sold in blocks, either fresh or vacuum-packed. Although it has a bland flavor, it readily absorbs the flavors of spices and herbs.

Serve these bite-size
chicken appetizers warm
as a snack, with drinks,
or cold for a picnic or
lunch-time treat.

Chicken Balls *with* Sauce

SERVES 4

3 tbsp vegetable oil

2 large skinless, boneless chicken breasts, cut
   into 3/4-inch/2-cm pieces

2 shallots, chopped finely

1 celery stalk, chopped finely

1 garlic clove, crushed

2 tbsp light soy sauce

1 small egg, beaten

1 bunch scallions, cut into 2-inch/
   5-cm lengths

salt and pepper

scallion tassels, to garnish

dipping sauce

3 tbsp dark soy sauce

1 tbsp rice wine

1 tsp sesame seeds

1 Heat half of the oil in a wok or large, heavy-based skillet and cook the chicken over a high heat for 2–3 minutes, until golden. Remove the chicken from the pan with a slotted spoon; set aside.

2 Add the shallots, celery, and garlic to the pan and cook for 1–2 minutes, until softened, but not browned.

3 Place the chicken, shallots, celery, and garlic in a food processor and process until finely ground. Add 1 tablespoon of the light soy sauce, just enough egg to make a fairly firm mixture, and season with salt and pepper.

4 Make the dipping sauce by mixing together the dark soy sauce, rice wine, and sesame seeds; set aside.

5 Shape the chicken mixture into 16–18 walnut-sized balls. Heat the remaining oil in the wok and cook the balls in small batches for 4–5 minutes, until golden brown. As each batch is cooked drain on paper towels and keep hot.

6 Cook the scallions for 1–2 minutes, until they begin to soften, then stir in the remaining light soy sauce. Serve the chicken balls and dipping sauce on a platter, garnished with the scallion tassels.

NUTRITION

Calories *214*; Sugars *29 g*; Protein *20 g*;
Carbohydrate *5 g*; Fat *13 g*; Saturates *2 g*

easy

10 mins

25 mins

This tasty Chinese appetizer is not all that it seems—the "seaweed" is in fact bok choy, which is fried, salted, and tossed with pine nuts.

Crispy Seaweed

1 Heat the peanut oil in a preheated wok or large, heavy-based skillet.

2 Carefully add the bok choy to the wok and cook for about 30 seconds, or until they shrivel up and become crispy. (You will probably need to do this in several batches, depending on the size of your wok.)

3 Remove the crispy "seaweed" from the wok with a slotted spoon and drain on paper towels.

4 Transfer the "seaweed" to a large bowl and toss with the salt, sugar, and pine nuts. Serve immediately on warm serving plates.

SERVES 4

3½ cups peanut oil, for deep-frying
2 lb 4 oz/1 kg bok choy, shredded
1 tsp salt
1 tbsp superfine sugar
2½ tbsp toasted pine nuts

NUTRITION
Calories *214*; Sugars *14 g*; Protein *6 g*;
Carbohydrate *15 g*; Fat *15 g*; Saturates *2 g*

⭐ very easy

🕐 10 mins

🕐 5 mins

🧑‍🍳 **COOK'S TIP**

If bok choy is unavailable, use Savoy cabbage instead, drying the leaves thoroughly before frying.

This makes a substantial appetizer, light lunch or supper dish. Serve with a colorful, crisp salad.

Thai-Stuffed Omelet

SERVES 4

2 garlic cloves, chopped
4 black peppercorns
4 sprigs fresh cilantro
2 tbsp vegetable oil
7 oz/200 g ground pork
2 scallions, chopped
1 large, firm tomato, chopped
6 large eggs
1 tbsp fish sauce
¼ tsp ground turmeric
mixed salad greens, to serve

1 Place the garlic, peppercorns, and cilantro in a pestle and mortar and crush to make a smooth paste.

2 Heat 1 tablespoon of the oil in a preheated wok or large, heavy-based skillet over a medium heat. Add the paste and cook for 1–2 minutes, until it just changes color.

3 Stir in the pork and cook until it is lightly browned. Add the scallions and tomato, and cook for another minute, then remove from the heat.

4 Heat the remaining oil in a small, heavy-based skillet. Beat the eggs with the fish sauce and turmeric, then pour a quarter of the egg mixture into the pan. As the mixture begins to set, stir lightly to ensure that all the liquid egg is set.

5 Spoon a quarter of the pork mixture down the center of the omelet, then fold the sides inward toward the center, enclosing the filling. Make 3 more omelets with the remaining egg and fill with the pork mixture.

6 Slide the omelets on to serving plates and serve with mixed salad greens.

NUTRITION
Calories 250; Sugars 1 g; Protein 21 g;
Carbohydrate 2 g; Fat 18 g; Saturates 4 g

⭐ very easy
🕐 10 mins
🕐 25 mins

👨‍🍳 **COOK'S TIP**

If you prefer, spread half of the pork mixture evenly over 1 omelet, then place a second omelet on top, without folding. Cut into slim wedges to serve.

These small fish cakes are quick to make and are delicious served with a fresh chile dip.

Thai-Style Fish Cakes

1 Place the cod pieces in a food processor with the fish sauce, chiles, garlic, lime leaves, cilantro, egg, and all-purpose flour. Process until finely chopped and spoon into a large mixing bowl.

2 Add the green beans to the cod mixture and mix well.

3 Divide the mixture into small balls. Flatten the balls between the palms of your hands to form rounds.

4 Heat a little oil in a preheated wok or large, heavy-based pan. Cook the fish cakes on both sides until brown and crispy on the outside.

5 Transfer the fish cakes to serving plates and serve hot.

SERVES 4

1 lb/450 g cod fillets, skinned and cut into bite-size pieces
2 tbsp fish sauce
2 fresh red Thai chiles, seeded and very chopped finely
2 garlic cloves, crushed
10 lime leaves, chopped finely
2 tbsp chopped fresh cilantro
1 large egg
scant $\frac{1}{4}$ cup all-purpose flour
3½ oz/100 g fine green beans, sliced finely
peanut oil, for frying

COOK'S TIP

Fish sauce is a salty, brown liquid which is a must for an authentic Thai flavor. It is available from Asian food stores or health food stores.

NUTRITION

Calories *214*; Sugars *14 g*; Protein *6 g*; Carbohydrate *15 g*; Fat *15 g*; Saturates *2 g*

⭐ very easy

🕐 10 mins

🕐 20 mins

These small shrimp bites are packed with the distinct flavors of lime and cilantro, and make a quick and tasty appetizer.

Shrimp Parcels

SERVES 4

1 tbsp sunflower oil
1 red bell pepper, seeded and sliced thinly
¾ cup beansprouts
finely grated zest and juice of 1 lime
1 fresh red chile, seeded and very
   chopped finely
1 tsp grated fresh gingerroot
8 oz/225 g peeled raw shrimp
1 tbsp fish sauce
½ tsp arrowroot
2 tbsp chopped fresh cilantro
8 sheets phyllo pastry
2 tbsp butter
2 tsp sesame oil
3 tbsp vegetable oil
chili sauce, to serve

1 Heat the sunflower oil in a preheated wok or large, heavy-based skillet. Add the red bell pepper and beansprouts and cook for 2 minutes, or until the vegetables have softened.

2 Remove the wok from the heat and add the lime zest and juice, red chile, ginger, and shrimp, stirring well.

3 Mix the fish sauce with the arrowroot and stir the mixture into the wok juices. Return the wok to the heat and cook, stirring, for 2 minutes, or until the juices thicken. Toss in the cilantro and mix well.

4 Lay the sheets of phyllo pastry out on a board. Melt the butter and sesame oil and brush each pastry sheet with the mixture.

5 Spoon a little of the shrimp filling on the bottom end of each sheet, fold over each side, and roll up to enclose the filling.

6 Heat the oil in a large wok. Cook the parcels, in batches, for 2–3 minutes, or until crisp and golden. Serve hot with a chili dipping sauce.

NUTRITION
Calories *305*; Sugars *2 g*; Protein *15 g*;
Carbohydrate *14 g*; Fat *21 g*; Saturates *8 g*

★★★   moderate
   15 mins
🕐   20 mins

🍳 **COOK'S TIP**

If using cooked shrimp, cook for 1 minute only, otherwise the shrimp will toughen.

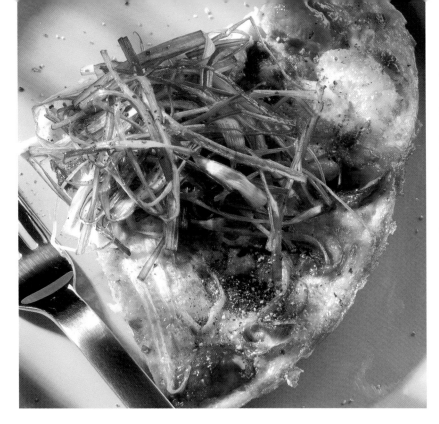

This is called *Foo Yung* in China and is a classic dish which may be flavored with any suitable ingredients you have to hand.

Shrimp Omelet

1 Heat the sunflower oil in a preheated wok or large, heavy based skillet. Add the leeks and cook for 3 minutes.

2 Rinse the shrimp under cold running water and then pat them dry with paper towels.

3 Mix together the cornstarch and salt in a large bowl.

4 Add the shrimp to the cornstarch and salt mixture and toss to coat all over.

5 Add the shrimp to the wok and cook for 2 minutes, or until the shrimp have changed color and are almost cooked through.

6 Add the mushrooms and beansprouts to the wok and cook for another 2 minutes.

7 Beat the eggs with the water. Pour the egg mixture into the wok and cook until the egg sets, carefully turning over once. Turn the omelet out on to a clean board, divide into 4 and serve hot, garnished with deep-fried leeks, if using.

SERVES 4

3 tbsp sunflower oil
2 leeks, sliced
12 oz/350 g raw, peeled jumbo shrimp
4 tbsp cornstarch
1 tsp salt
6 oz/175 g mushrooms, sliced
1¾ cups beansprouts
6 eggs
3 tbsp cold water
deep-fried leeks, to garnish (optional)

COOK'S TIP

If liked, divide the mixture into 4 once the initial cooking has taken place in step 6 and make 4 individual omelets.

NUTRITION
Calories *320*; Sugars *1 g*; Protein *31 g*; Carbohydrate *8 g*; Fat *18 g*; Saturates *4 g*

⭐⭐⭐   moderate

🕐   10 mins

🕐   10 mins

These are one of the most recognized and popular appetizers in Chinese restaurants in the Western world. They are also quick and easy to make at home.

Sesame Shrimp Toasts

SERVES 4

4 slices medium-thick sliced white bread, crusts removed (optional)
8 oz/225 g cooked, peeled shrimp
1 tbsp soy sauce
2 garlic cloves, crushed
1 tbsp sesame oil
1 egg
2 tbsp sesame seeds
oil, for deep-frying
sweet chile sauce, to serve

1 Place the shrimp, soy sauce, garlic, sesame oil, and egg in a food processor and blend to make a smooth paste.

2 Spread the shrimp paste evenly over the 4 slices of bread. Sprinkle the sesame seeds over the top of the shrimp mixture and press the seeds down with your hands so that they stick. Cut each slice into quarters.

3 Heat the oil in a preheated wok or large, heavy-based skillet and deep-fry the toasts, sesame seed-side up, for 4–5 minutes, or until golden and crispy.

4 Remove the toasts with a slotted spoon and transfer to paper towels and let drain thoroughly.

5 Serve the sesame shrimp toasts warm with sweet chile sauce for dipping.

NUTRITION
Calories *237*; Sugars *1 g*; Protein *18 g*;
Carbohydrate *15 g*; Fat *12 g*; Saturates *2 g*

easy

5 mins

10 mins

 COOK'S TIP

Add 2 chopped scallions to the shrimp mixture at the end of step 1 for added flavor and crunch.

Shrimp are marinated in a soy sauce mixture, then coated in a light batter and served with a delicious sweet-and-sour dip.

Sweet *and* Sour Shrimp

1 Using tweezers, de-vein the shrimp, then flatten them with a large knife.

2 Place the shrimp in a dish and add the ginger, garlic, scallions, dry sherry, sesame oil, and soy sauce. Cover them with plastic wrap and let them marinate for 30 minutes.

3 Make the batter by beating the egg whites until thick. Fold in the cornstarch and all-purpose flour to form a light batter.

4 Place all of the sauce ingredients in a pan and bring to a boil. Reduce the heat and let simmer for 10 minutes.

5 Remove the shrimp from the marinade and dip them into the batter to coat.

6 Heat the vegetable oil in a preheated wok or large skillet until almost smoking. Reduce the heat and cook the shrimp for 3–4 minutes, until crisp and golden brown.

7 Garnish the shrimp with shredded scallion and serve with the sauce.

S E R V E S   4

16 large raw shrimp, peeled
1 tsp grated fresh gingerroot
1 garlic clove, crushed
2 scallions, sliced, plus extra to garnish
2 tbsp dry sherry
2 tsp sesame oil
1 tbsp light soy sauce
vegetable oil, for deep-frying

batter
4 egg whites
4 tbsp cornstarch
2 tbsp all-purpose flour

sauce
2 tbsp each tomato paste and lemon juice
3 tbsp white wine vinegar
4 tsp light soy sauce
3 tbsp light brown sugar
1 green bell pepper, seeded and sliced thinly
½ tsp chile sauce
1¼ cups vegetable bouillon
2 tsp cornstarch

NUTRITION
Calories *294*; Sugars *11 g*; Protein *14 g*;
Fat *12 g*; Carbohydrate *34 g*; Saturates *2 g*

★★★★ challenging
🕐 40 mins
🕐 20 mins

Chicken wings make an ideal appetizer, since they are small and perfect for eating with the fingers.

Honeyed Chicken Wings

SERVES 4

1 lb/450 g chicken wings
2 tbsp peanut oil
2 tbsp light soy sauce
2 tbsp Peking sauce
2 tbsp clear honey
2 garlic cloves, crushed
1 tsp sesame seeds

marinade
1 dried red chili
1/2–1 tsp chili powder
1/2–1 tsp ground ginger
finely grated zest of 1 lime

1 To make the marinade, crush the dried chili with a pestle and mortar. Mix together the crushed dried chili, chili powder, ground ginger, and lime zest in a small mixing bowl.

2 Thoroughly rub the spice mixture into the chicken wings with your fingertips. Let stand for at least 2 hours in the refrigerator to allow the flavors to penetrate the chicken wings.

3 Heat the peanut oil in a wok or large, heavy-based skillet.

4 Add the chicken wings and cook, turning frequently, for about 10–12 minutes, until golden and crisp. Drain off any excess oil.

5 Add the soy sauce, Peking sauce, honey, garlic, and sesame seeds to the wok, turning the chicken wings to coat.

6 Reduce the heat and cook for 20–25 minutes, turning the chicken wings frequently, until completely cooked through. Serve hot.

NUTRITION
Calories 131; Sugars 4 g; Protein 10 g;
Carbohydrate 4 g; Fat 8 g; Saturates 2 g

easy
2 hrs 5 mins
40 mins

🍳 **COOK'S TIP**

Make the dish in advance and freeze the chicken wings. Thaw thoroughly, cover with aluminum foil, and heat right through in a moderate oven.

The dough used in this recipe may also be wrapped around chicken, pork, or shrimp, or sweet fillings, as an alternative.

Steamed Duck Buns

1 Place the duck breast in a large bowl. Mix together the brown sugar, soy sauce, honey, and Peking sauce. Pour the mixture over the duck and marinate for 20 minutes.

2 Remove the duck from the marinade and cook on a rack set over a roasting pan in a preheated oven, at 400°F/200°C for 35–40 minutes, or until cooked through. Let cool, remove the meat from the bones, and cube.

3 Heat the vegetable oil in a preheated wok or large, heavy-based skillet until really hot. Add the leek, garlic, and ginger, and cook for 3 minutes. Mix with the duck meat.

4 Strain the flour into a large bowl. Mix the yeast, superfine sugar, and warm water in a separate bowl and let stand in a warm place for 15 minutes.

5 Pour the yeast mixture into the flour, together with the warm milk, mixing to form a firm dough. Knead the dough on a floured counter for 5 minutes. Roll into a sausage shape, 1-inch/2.5-cm in diameter. Cut into 16 pieces, cover, and let stand for 20–25 minutes.

6 Flatten the dough pieces into 4-inch/10-cm circles. Place a spoonful of filling in the center of each, draw up the sides to form a "moneybag" shape and twist to seal.

7 Place the dumplings on a clean, damp dish cloth in the base of a steamer, cover, and steam for 20 minutes. Serve immediately.

SERVES 4

10½ oz/300 g duck breast
1 tbsp brown sugar
1 tbsp light soy sauce
2 tbsp clear honey
1 tbsp Peking sauce
1 tbsp vegetable oil
1 leek, chopped finely
1 garlic clove, crushed
1 tsp grated fresh gingerroot

dough
generous 2 cups all-purpose flour
½ oz/15 g dry yeast
1 tsp superfine sugar
2 tbsp warm water
¾ cup warm milk

NUTRITION
Calories *307*; Sugars *11 g*; Protein *17 g*;
Carbohydrate *50 g*; Fat *6 g*; Saturates *1 g*

★★★★ challenging
🕐 1 hr 30 mins
🕐 1 hr

This classic Chinese dish
is very popular in the West.
Serve hot or chilled with
a soy sauce or Peking dip.

Spring Rolls

S E R V E S   4

6 oz/175 g cooked pork, chopped
2¾ oz/75 g cooked chicken, chopped
1 tsp each of light soy sauce, brown sugar,
 sesame oil, and vegetable oil
2¼ cups beansprouts
1 oz/25 g canned bamboo shoots, chopped
1 green bell pepper, seeded and chopped
2 scallions, sliced
1 tsp cornstarch
2 tsp water
vegetable oil, for deep-frying

skins
scant 1 cup all-purpose flour
5 tbsp cornstarch
2 cups water
3 tbsp vegetable oil

N U T R I T I O N
Calories *442*; Sugars *4 g*; Protein *23 g*;
Carbohydrate *42 g*; Fat *21 g*; Saturates *3 g*

⭐⭐⭐⭐ challenging
🕐   45 mins
🕐   30 mins

1 Mix together the pork, chicken, soy sauce, sugar, and sesame oil. Cover and marinate in the refrigerator for 30 minutes.

2 Heat the vegetable oil in a preheated wok or large, heavy-based skillet. Add the beansprouts, bamboo shoots, bell pepper, and scallions to the wok and cook for 2–3 minutes. Add the meat and the marinade to the wok and cook for 2–3 minutes.

3 Blend the cornstarch with the water and stir the mixture into the wok. Let cool completely.

4 To make the skins, mix the flour and cornstarch and gradually stir in the water, to make a smooth batter.

5 Heat a small, oiled skillet. Swirl one-eighth of the batter over the bottom and cook for 2–3 minutes. Repeat with the remaining batter. Cover the skins with a damp dish cloth, while cooking the remaining skins.

6 Spread out the skins and spoon one-eighth of the filling along the center of each. Brush the edges with water and fold in the sides, then roll up.

7 Heat the oil for deep-frying in a wok to 350°F/180°C. Cook the spring rolls, in batches, for 2–3 minutes, or until golden and crisp. Remove from the oil with a slotted spoon, drain and serve immediately.

This classic dim sum dish is adaptable to almost any filling of your choice. Here, a traditional mixture of pork and bok choy is used.

Pancake Rolls

1 Heat the oil in a preheated wok or large, heavy-based skillet. Add the garlic and cook for 30 seconds. Add the pork and cook for 2–3 minutes, until lightly colored.

2 Add the bok choy, soy sauce, and sesame oil to the wok and cook for 2–3 minutes. Remove from the heat and let cool.

3 Spread out the spring roll skins on a counter and spoon 2 tablespoons of the pork mixture along one edge of each. Roll the skin over once and fold in the sides. Roll up completely to make a sausage shape, brushing the edges with a little water to seal. Set the pancake rolls aside for 10 minutes to seal firmly.

4 To make the chile sauce, heat the sugar, vinegar, and water in a small pan, stirring until the sugar dissolves. Bring the mixture to a boil and boil rapidly until a light syrup forms. Remove from the heat and stir in the red chiles. Let the sauce cool before serving.

5 Heat the oil for deep-frying in a wok until almost smoking. Reduce the heat slightly and cook the pancake rolls, in batches if necessary, for 3–4 minutes, until golden brown. Remove from the oil with a slotted spoon and drain on paper towels. Serve on a warm serving plate with the chile sauce.

SERVES 4

4 tsp vegetable oil
1–2 garlic cloves, crushed
8 oz/225 g ground pork
8 oz/225 g bok choy, shredded
41/2 tsp light soy sauce
1/2 tsp sesame oil
8 spring roll skins, 10-inch/
　25-cm square, thawed if frozen
oil, for deep-frying

chile sauce

generous 1/4 cup superfine sugar
scant 1/4 cup rice wine vinegar
2 tbsp water
2 fresh red chiles, chopped finely

NUTRITION
Calories *488*; Sugars *19 g*; Protein *16 g*;
Carbohydrate *55 g*; Fat *24 g*; Saturates *4 g*

✪✪✪✪　challenging
　　　　20 mins
　　　　20 mins

Poultry *and* Meat

Meat is expensive in Far Eastern countries and is eaten in smaller proportions than in the Western world. However, when meat is used, it is done so to its full potential—it is marinated or spiced and combined with other delicious native flavorings to create a wide array of mouthwatering dishes. In Malaysia, a wide variety of spicy meats is offered, reflecting the many ethnic origins of the population. In China, poultry, lamb, beef, or pork are stir-fried or steamed in the wok and combined with sauces and seasonings such as soy, black bean, and oyster sauce. In Japan, meat is usually marinated and quickly stir-fried in a wok over a very high heat or simmered in miso stock. Thai dishes use meat that is leaner and more flavorsome due to its "free-range" rearing.

The orange adds color and piquancy to this refreshing dish, which complements the chicken well.

Stir-Fried Ginger Chicken

SERVES 4

2 tbsp sunflower oil
1 onion, sliced
2 carrots, cut into thin sticks
1 garlic clove, crushed
12 oz/350 g skinless, boneless chicken
  breasts, cut into thin strips
2 tbsp grated fresh gingerroot
1 tsp ground ginger
4 tbsp sweet sherry
1 tbsp tomato paste
1 tbsp raw brown sugar
generous ⅓ cup orange juice
1 tsp cornstarch
1 orange, peeled and segmented
fresh snipped chives, to garnish

1 Heat the oil in a preheated wok or large, heavy-based skillet. Add the onion, carrots, and garlic and cook over a high heat for 3 minutes, or until the vegetables have softened.

2 Add the chicken to the wok with the fresh and ground ginger. Cook for another 10 minutes, or until the chicken is well cooked through and golden in color.

3 Mix together the sherry, tomato paste, sugar, orange juice, and cornstarch in a bowl. Stir the mixture into the wok and heat through until the mixture bubbles and the juices start to thicken.

4 Add the orange segments and carefully toss to mix.

5 Transfer the stir-fried chicken to warm serving bowls and garnish with freshly snipped chives. Serve immediately.

NUTRITION
Calories *289*; Sugars *15 g*; Protein *20 g*;
Carbohydrate *17 g*; Fat *9 g*; Saturates *2 g*

★★★   moderate

🕐   10 mins

🕐   20 mins

🌀 **COOK'S TIP**

Make sure that you do not continue cooking the dish once the orange segments have been added in step 4, otherwise they will break up.

Okra are slightly bitter. The pineapple and coconut in this recipe offsets them in both color and flavor.

Coconut Chicken Curry

1 Heat the oil in a preheated wok or large, heavy-based skillet. Add the chicken to the wok, and cook until evenly browned.

2 Add the okra, onion, and garlic to the wok and cook for a further 2–3 minutes, stirring constantly.

3 Mix the curry paste with the chicken bouillon and lemon juice and pour the mixture into the wok, then bring to a boil. Reduce the heat, cover, and let simmer for 30 minutes.

4 Stir the grated coconut into the curry and cook for about 5 minutes.

5 Add the pineapple, yogurt, and cilantro and cook for 2 minutes, stirring. Serve with rice and garnish with the cilantro.

SERVES 4

1 lb/450 g skinless, boneless chicken thighs or breasts, cut into bite-size pieces
2 tbsp sunflower oil
1 cup okra, tops trimmed
1 large onion, sliced
2 garlic cloves, crushed
3 tbsp mild curry paste
1 ¼ cups chicken bouillon
1 tbsp fresh lemon juice
½ cup coarsely grated creamed coconut
1 ¼ cups cubed fresh or canned pineapple
⅔ cup thick, unsweetened yogurt
2 tbsp chopped fresh cilantro
freshly boiled rice, to serve
fresh cilantro sprigs, to garnish

NUTRITION
Calories *456*; Sugars *21 g*; Protein *29 g*; Carbohydrate *22 g*; Fat *29 g*; Saturates *17 g*

moderate

5 mins

45 mins

🍳 **COOK'S TIP**

Score around the top of the okra with a knife before cooking to release the sticky, glue-like substance which is bitter in taste.

Yellow bean sauce is available from large food stores. Try to buy a chunky sauce, rather than a smooth one for texture.

Cashew Chicken

SERVES 4

2 tbsp vegetable oil
1 lb/450 g skinless, boneless chicken breasts, cut into bite-size pieces
1 red onion, sliced
6 oz/175 g flat mushrooms, sliced
1 cup cashews
2 3/4 oz/75 g jar yellow bean sauce
fresh cilantro, to garnish
egg fried rice or plain boiled rice, to serve

1 Heat the vegetable oil in a preheated wok or large, heavy-based skillet.

2 Add the chicken to the wok and cook for 5 minutes.

3 Add the red onion and mushrooms to the wok and continue to stir-fry for another 5 minutes.

4 Place the cashews on a cookie sheet and toast under a preheated medium broiler until just browning—toasting nuts brings out their flavor.

5 Toss the toasted cashews into the wok with the yellow bean sauce and heat through. Allow the sauce to bubble for 2–3 minutes.

6 Transfer the stir-fry to warm serving bowls and garnish with fresh cilantro. Serve hot with egg fried rice or plain boiled rice.

NUTRITION

Calories *398*; Sugars *2 g*; Protein *31 g*;
Carbohydrate *8 g*; Fat *27 g*; Saturates *4 g*

easy

10 mins

15 mins

🍳 **COOK'S TIP**

Chicken thighs could be used instead of the chicken breasts for a more economical dish.

This is on nearly everyone's list of favorite Chinese dishes, and it is so simple to make. Serve with lightly cooked vegetables for a truly delicious meal.

Lemon Chicken

1 Heat the oil for deep-frying in a preheated wok or large, heavy-based pan to 350°F/180°C, or until a cube of bread browns in 30 seconds.

2 Reduce the heat and cook the chicken for 3–4 minutes, until cooked through.

3 Remove the chicken with a slotted spoon, set aside, and keep warm. Drain the oil from the wok.

4 To make the sauce, mix the cornstarch with 2 tablespoons of the water to make a paste.

5 Pour the lemon juice and remaining water into the wok.

6 Add the sweet sherry and superfine sugar and bring to a boil, stirring until the sugar has completely dissolved.

7 Stir in the cornstarch mixture and return to a boil. Reduce the heat and simmer, stirring constantly, for 2–3 minutes, until the sauce has thickened and cleared.

8 Transfer the chicken to a warm serving plate and pour the sauce over. Garnish the chicken with the lemon and scallion and serve immediately.

SERVES 4

vegetable oil, for deep-frying
1 lb 7 oz/650 g skinless, boneless chicken, cut into strips

sauce
1 tbsp cornstarch
6 tbsp cold water
3 tbsp fresh lemon juice
2 tbsp sweet sherry
½ tsp superfine sugar

to garnish
lemon slices
shredded scallion

NUTRITION
Calories *272*; Sugars *1 g*; Protein *36 g*; Carbohydrate *5 g*; Fat *11 g*; Saturates *2 g*

⊛⊛⊛ moderate
🕐 10 mins
🕐 15 mins

👨‍🍳 COOK'S TIP

If you prefer to use chicken portions rather than strips, cook them in the oil, covered, over a low heat for about 30 minutes, or until cooked through.

Chop suey is a well known and popular dish based on beansprouts and soy sauce with a meat or vegetable flavoring.

Chicken Chop Suey

SERVES 4

4 tbsp light soy sauce
2 tsp brown sugar
1 lb 2 oz /500 g skinless, boneless chicken
  breasts, cut into thin strips
3 tbsp vegetable oil
2 onions, quartered
2 garlic cloves, crushed
3½ cups beansprouts
3 tsp sesame oil
1 tbsp cornstarch
3 tbsp water
scant 2 cups chicken bouillon
shredded leek, to garnish

1 Mix the soy sauce and sugar together, stirring until the sugar has dissolved.

2 Place the chicken in a shallow dish and spoon the soy mixture over it, turning to coat. Marinate in the refrigerator for 20 minutes.

3 Heat the oil in a preheated wok or large, heavy-based skillet and cook the chicken for 2–3 minutes, until golden brown. Add the onions and garlic and cook for another 2 minutes. Add the beansprouts, cook for 4–5 minutes, then add the sesame oil.

4 Mix the cornstarch and water to form a smooth paste. Pour the bouillon into the wok, add the cornstarch paste and bring to a boil, stirring until the sauce has thickened and cleared. Serve, garnished with the leek.

NUTRITION
Calories *140*; Sugars *3 g*; Protein *3 g*;
Carbohydrate *20 g*; Fat *17 g*; Saturates *1 g*

⭐⭐⭐ moderate

🕐 25 mins

🕐 15 mins

🧑‍🍳 **COOK'S TIP**

This recipe may be made with strips of lean steak, pork, or mixed vegetables. Change the type of bouillon accordingly.

Chicken drumsticks are cooked in a delicious sauce and served with deep-fried basil for color and flavor.

Chicken *with* Chile *and* Basil

1 Remove the skin from the chicken drumsticks, if desired. Make 3 slashes in each drumstick. Brush the drumsticks with the soy sauce.

2 Heat the sunflower oil in a preheated wok or large, heavy-based skillet. Cook the drumsticks for 20 minutes, turning frequently, until cooked through.

3 Add the chile, carrot, and celery to the wok and cook for another 5 minutes. Stir in the chile sauce, cover and allow to bubble gently while preparing the basil leaves.

4 Heat a little oil in a heavy based pan. Carefully add the basil leaves—stand well away from the pan and protect your hand with a dish cloth as they may spit a little. Cook the basil leaves for about 30 seconds, or until they begin to curl up, but not brown. Let the leaves drain on paper towels.

5 Arrange the cooked chicken, vegetables, and pan juices on a warm serving plate, garnish with the deep-fried crispy basil leaves and serve immediately.

SERVES 4

8 chicken drumsticks
2 tbsp soy sauce
1 tbsp sunflower oil
1 fresh red chile, seeded and chopped
1 large carrot, cut into thin sticks
6 celery stalks, cut into sticks
3 tbsp sweet chili sauce
oil, for cooking
about 50 fresh basil leaves

COOK'S TIP

Basil has a very strong flavor, which is perfect with chicken and Chinese flavorings. You could use baby spinach instead of the basil, if you prefer.

NUTRITION
Calories *196*; Sugars *2 g*; Protein *23 g*;
Carbohydrate *3 g*; Fat *10 g*; Saturates *2 g*

⊛⊛⊛ moderate
◔ 10 mins
◕ 30 mins

In this recipe, the chicken is brushed with a glaze and deep-fried until golden. It is a little time-consuming, but well worth the effort.

Crispy Chicken

SERVES 4

3 lb 5 oz/1.5 kg oven-ready chicken
2 tbsp clear honey
2 tsp Chinese five-spice powder
2 tbsp rice wine vinegar
3 ½ cups vegetable oil, for deep-frying
chili sauce, to serve

1 Rinse the chicken inside and out under cold running water and pat dry with paper towels.

2 Bring a large pan of water to a boil, then remove from the heat. Place the chicken in the water, cover, and set aside for 20 minutes.

3 Remove the chicken from the water and pat dry with paper towels. Cool the chicken and let chill in the refrigerator overnight.

4 To make the glaze, mix together the honey, Chinese five-spice powder, and rice wine vinegar in a small bowl. Brush some of the glaze over the chicken and return it to the refrigerator for 20 minutes.

5 Repeat this process of glazing and refrigerating the chicken until all of the glaze has been used up. Return the chicken to the refrigerator for at least 2 hours after the final coating.

6 Using a cleaver or heavy knife, open the chicken out by splitting it down the center through the breast, and then cut each half into 4 pieces.

7 Heat the oil for deep-frying in a preheated wok or large pan until almost smoking. Reduce the heat and cook each piece of chicken for 5–7 minutes, until golden and cooked through. Remove from the oil with a slotted spoon and drain on paper towels. Serve hot with a little chili sauce.

NUTRITION

Calories *283*; Sugars *8 g*; Protein *29 g*; Carbohydrate *8 g*; Fat *15 g*; Saturates *3 g*

✪✪✪✪ challenging

15 hrs

35 mins

This quick dish has many variations, but this version includes the classic combination of peanuts, chicken, and chiles.

Spicy Peanut Chicken

1 Heat the peanut oil in a preheated wok or large, heavy-based skillet.

2 Add the peanuts to the wok and cook for 1 minute. Remove the peanuts with a slotted spoon and set aside.

3 Add the chicken to the wok and cook for 1–2 minutes.

4 Stir in the chile and green bell pepper and cook for 1 minute. Remove the chicken, chile, and green bell pepper from the wok with a slotted spoon and set aside.

5 Put half of the peanuts in a food processor and process until almost smooth. If necessary, add a little bouillon to form a softer paste. Alternatively, place them in a plastic bag and crush them with a rolling pin.

6 To make the sauce, add the chicken bouillon, Chinese rice wine, light soy sauce, light brown sugar, garlic, ginger, and rice wine vinegar to the wok.

7 Heat the sauce without boiling and stir in the peanut paste, remaining peanuts, chicken, red chile, and green bell pepper. Mix well until all the ingredients are thoroughly combined.

8 Sprinkle the sesame oil into the wok, stir and cook for 1 minute. Transfer the chicken to a warm serving dish and serve hot with fried rice.

SERVES 4

2 tbsp peanut oil
1 cup shelled peanuts
10½ oz/300 g skinless, boneless chicken breast, cut into 1-inch/2.5-cm pieces
1 fresh red chile, sliced
1 green bell pepper, seeded and cut into strips

sauce

⅔ cup chicken bouillon
1 tbsp Chinese rice wine or dry sherry
1 tbsp light soy sauce
1½ tsp light brown sugar
2 garlic cloves, crushed
1 tsp grated fresh gingerroot
1 tsp rice wine vinegar
1 tsp sesame oil

NUTRITION
Calories 342; Sugars 3 g; Protein 25 g; Carbohydrate 6 g; Fat 24 g; Saturates 5 g

✪✪✪✪ challenging

5 mins

10 mins

This is a refreshing dish suitable for a summer meal or light lunch.

Chinese Chicken Salad

SERVES 4

8 oz/225 g skinless, boneless chicken breasts
2 tsp light soy sauce
1 tsp each of sesame oil and sesame seeds
2 tbsp vegetable oil
1¼ cups beansprouts
1 red bell pepper, seeded and thinly sliced
1 carrot, cut into very thin sticks
3 baby corn cobs, sliced

sauce
2 tsp rice wine vinegar
1 tbsp light soy sauce
dash of chili oil

to garnish
fresh chives
carrot sticks

1 Place the chicken breasts in a shallow glass dish.

2 Mix together the soy sauce and sesame oil and pour the mixture over the chicken. Sprinkle with the sesame seeds and let stand for 20 minutes, turning the chicken occasionally.

3 Remove the chicken from the marinade and cut the meat into thin slices.

4 Heat the vegetable oil in a preheated wok or large, heavy-based skillet. Add the chicken and cook for 4–5 minutes, until cooked through and golden brown on both sides. Remove the chicken from the wok with a slotted spoon, set aside and let cool.

5 Add the beansprouts, red bell pepper, carrot, and baby corn cobs to the wok and cook for 2–3 minutes. Remove from the wok with a slotted spoon, set aside and let the mixture cool.

6 To make the sauce, mix together all the ingredients until well blended.

7 Arrange the chicken and vegetables together on a serving plate. Spoon the sauce over the salad, garnish with chives and carrot sticks and serve.

NUTRITION
Calories *162*; Sugars *3 g*; Protein *15 g*;
Carbohydrate 5g; Fat *10 g*; Saturates *2 g*

easy

25 mins

10 mins

Egg noodles are the ideal accompaniment to this quick dish, because they can be cooked quickly while the pan-fry sizzles.

Speedy Peanut Pan-Fry

1 Cook the noodles in a pan of lightly salted boiling water for 3–4 minutes. Drain the noodles well.

2 Meanwhile, heat the corn oil and sesame oil in a preheated wok or large, heavy-based skillet and fry the chicken over a fairly high heat for 1 minute.

3 Add the zucchini, corn, and mushrooms, and cook for 5 minutes.

4 Add the beansprouts, peanut butter, soy sauce, lime or lemon juice, and season with pepper, then cook for a further 2 minutes.

5 Scatter the roasted peanuts over the noodles and serve with the zucchini and mushroom mixture. Garnish with sprigs of fresh cilantro.

SERVES 4

9 oz/250 g dried thread egg noodles
2 tbsp corn oil
1 tbsp sesame oil
8 skinless, boneless chicken thighs
    or 4 breasts, sliced thinly
10½ oz/300 g zucchini, sliced thinly
9 oz/250 g baby corn cobs, sliced thinly
10½ oz/300 g white mushrooms,
    sliced thinly
3½ cups beansprouts
4 tbsp smooth peanut butter
2 tbsp soy sauce
2 tbsp lime or lemon juice
generous ½ cup roasted peanuts
salt and pepper
sprigs of fresh cilantro, to garnish

NUTRITION
Calories 563; Sugars 7 g; Protein 45 g;
Carbohydrate 22 g; Fat 33 g; Saturates 7 g

⭐⭐ easy
🕐 5 mins
🕐 15 mins

🧑‍🍳 COOK'S TIP

Try serving this pan-fry with flat rice noodles as an alternative. These broad, pale, translucent ribbon noodles are made from ground rice.

This stir-fry uses the minimum of fat, making it a quick and healthy meal.

Chicken *and* Corn Sauté

SERVES 4

2 tbsp sunflower oil

4 skinless, boneless chicken breasts, cut into thin strips

9 oz/250 g baby corn cobs, halved lengthwise

9 oz/250 g snow peas

1 tbsp sherry vinegar

1 tbsp clear honey

1 tbsp light soy sauce

1 tbsp sunflower seeds

pepper

boiled Chinese egg noodles or rice, to serve

1 Heat the sunflower oil in a preheated wok or large, heavy-based skillet.

2 Add the chicken and cook over a fairly high heat, stirring, for 1 minute.

3 Add the baby corn cobs and snow peas and cook over a moderate heat for 5–8 minutes, until evenly cooked. The chicken should be cooked through and vegetables still slightly crunchy.

4 Mix together the sherry vinegar, honey, and soy sauce in a small bowl.

5 Stir the vinegar mixture into the pan with the sunflower seeds. Season well with pepper. Cook, stirring, for 1 minute.

6 Serve the dish hot with Chinese egg noodles or rice.

NUTRITION

Calories *280*; Sugars *7 g*; Protein *31 g*; Carbohydrate *9 g*; Fat *11 g*; Saturates *2 g*

easy

5 mins

10 mins

🍳 **COOK'S TIP**

Rice wine vinegar or balsamic vinegar make a good substitute for the sherry vinegar.

A colorful, exotic mix of flavors that works surprisingly well. This dish is easy and quick to cook and is ideal for a mid-week family meal.

Chicken *and* Mango Stir-Fry

1 Mix together the ginger, garlic, and chile in a shallow dish, then add the chicken strips and turn to coat evenly.

2 Heat the oil in a preheated wok or large, heavy-based skillet over a high heat. Add the chicken and cook for 4–5 minutes, until light golden. Reduce the heat, add the red bell pepper and cook for 4–5 minutes, until softened.

3 Add the scallions, snow peas, and corn cobs and cook for another minute.

4 Mix together the soy sauce, rice wine, and sesame oil, and stir it into the wok. Add the mango and cook gently for 1 minute to heat thoroughly.

5 Season with salt and pepper to taste and serve immediately, garnished with snipped fresh chives.

SERVES 4

2 tsp fresh gingerroot, grated
1 garlic clove, crushed
1 small fresh red chile, seeded
6 skinless, boneless, chicken thighs, cut into thin strips
2 tbsp sunflower oil
1 large red bell pepper, seeded and sliced thinly diagonally
4 scallions, sliced thinly diagonally
7 oz/200 g snow peas, halved
3½ oz/100 g baby corn cobs, halved lengthwise
1 tbsp light soy sauce
3 tbsp rice wine or sherry
1 tsp sesame oil
1 large, ripe mango peeled, pitted and sliced thinly
salt and pepper
snipped chives, to garnish

NUTRITION

Calories *200*; Sugars *5 g*; Protein *23 g*; Carbohydrate *7 g*; Fat *6 g*; Saturates *1 g*

✪✪✪   moderate

🕐   10 mins

🕐   15 mins

Coconut adds a creamy texture and delicious flavor to this Thai-style stir-fry, which is spiked with fresh green chile.

Thai Stir-Fried Chicken

SERVES 4

3 tbsp sesame oil
12 oz/350 g skinless, boneless chicken breasts, sliced thinly
2 shallots, sliced
2 garlic cloves, chopped finely
2 tsp grated fresh gingerroot
1 fresh green chile, chopped finely
1 each red and green bell pepper, sliced thinly
3 zucchini, sliced thinly
2 tbsp ground almonds
1 tsp ground cinnamon
1 tbsp oyster sauce
¼ cup grated creamed coconut
salt and pepper

1 Heat the sesame oil in a preheated wok or large, heavy-based skillet. Add the chicken, season with salt and pepper, and cook for about 4 minutes.

2 Add the shallots, garlic, ginger, and chile, and cook for another 2 minutes.

3 Add the red and green bell peppers and zucchini and cook for about 1 minute.

4 Add the remaining ingredients and check the seasoning. Cook for 1 minute and serve immediately on warm serving plates.

NUTRITION
Calories *184*; Sugars *6 g*; Protein *24 g*;
Carbohydrate *8 g*; Fat *5 g*; Saturates *2 g*

⭐ very easy
🕐 15 mins
🕐 10 mins

🍳 **COOK'S TIP**

Creamed coconut is sold in blocks by superstores and Asian stores. It is a useful store-cupboard standby as it adds richness and depth of flavor.

This tasty chicken stir-fry is quick and easy to make and is full of fresh flavors and crunchy vegetables.

Chicken *with* Black Bean Sauce

1 Put the chicken in a bowl. Add the salt and cornstarch and cover with water, then mix well. Let stand in the refrigerator for 30 minutes.

2 Heat 1 tablespoon of the oil in a preheated wok or large, heavy-based skillet and cook the chicken for 4 minutes.

3 Remove the chicken using a slotted spoon and transfer to a warm serving dish and clean the wok.

4 Add the remaining oil to the wok and add the garlic, black bean sauce, red and green bell peppers, chile, mushrooms, onion, and scallions. Cook for 2 minutes, then return the chicken to the wok.

5 Add the seasoning ingredients, cook for 3 minutes and thicken with a little of the cornstarch blend. Serve immediately with fresh noodles.

SERVES 4

15 oz/425 g skinless, boneless chicken breasts, sliced thinly
pinch each of salt and cornstarch
2 tbsp oil
1 garlic clove, crushed
1 tbsp black bean sauce
1 each small red and green bell pepper, seeded and cut into strips
1 fresh red chile, chopped finely
2¾ oz/75 g mushrooms, sliced
1 onion, chopped
6 scallions, chopped
boiled fresh egg noodles, to serve

seasoning
½ tsp each of salt and sugar
3 tbsp chicken bouillon
1 tbsp dark soy sauce
2 tbsp each of beef bouillon and Chinese rice wine
1 tsp cornstarch, blended with a little Chinese rice wine

NUTRITION
Calories *184*; Sugars *6 g*; Protein *24 g*; Carbohydrate *8 g*; Fat *5 g*; Saturates *2 g*

✪✪✪   moderate
◔   40 mins
◕   10 mins

Traditional Thanksgiving ingredients are given a Chinese twist in this stir-fry, which contains cranberries, ginger, chestnuts, and soy sauce.

Turkey *with* Cranberry Glaze

SERVES 4

2 tbsp sunflower oil
1 skinless, boneless turkey breast, sliced thinly
2 tbsp preserved ginger, chopped finely
½ cup fresh or frozen cranberries
3½ oz/100 g canned chestnuts
4 tbsp cranberry sauce
3 tbsp light soy sauce
salt and pepper

1 Heat the sunflower oil in a preheated wok or large, heavy-based skillet.

2 Add the turkey to the wok and cook for 5 minutes, or until cooked through.

3 Add the ginger and the cranberries to the wok and cook for 2–3 minutes, or until the cranberries have softened.

4 Add the chestnuts, cranberry sauce, and soy sauce, season to taste with salt and pepper, and allow to bubble for 2–3 minutes.

5 Transfer the turkey stir-fry to warm serving dishes and serve immediately.

NUTRITION

Calories *167*; Sugars *11 g*; Protein *8 g*;
Carbohydrate *20 g*; Fat *7 g*; Saturates *1 g*

easy

5 mins

15 mins

🍳 COOK'S TIP

It is very important that the wok is very hot before you begin to cook. Test by holding your hand flat about 3-inches/7.5-cm above the bottom of the interior—you should be able to feel the heat radiating from it.

Chinese five-spice powder gives a lovely flavor to this sliced duck, while the chile adds a slight kick.

Duck *in* Spicy Sauce

1 Heat the oil in a preheated wok or large, heavy-based skillet. Reduce the heat slightly, add the ginger, garlic, chile, and duck, and cook for 2–3 minutes. Remove the duck from the wok and set aside.

2 Add the vegetables to the wok and cook for 2–3 minutes. Pour off any excess oil from the wok and push the vegetables to one side.

3 Return the duck to the wok and pour in the bouillon. Add the Chinese five-spice powder, stir in the Chinese rice wine, and cook over a low heat for 15 minutes, or until the duck is tender.

4 Blend the cornstarch with the water to form a paste and stir into the wok with the sesame oil. Bring to a boil, stirring until the sauce has thickened and cleared. Transfer the duck and spicy sauce to a warm serving dish and serve immediately.

SERVES 4

1 tbsp vegetable oil

1 tsp grated fresh gingerroot

1 garlic clove, crushed

1 fresh red chile, chopped

12 oz/350 g skinless, boneless duck meat, cut into strips

4$\frac{1}{2}$ oz/125 g cauliflower florets

2 oz/55 g snow peas

2 oz/55 g baby corn cobs, halved lengthwise

1$\frac{1}{4}$ cups chicken bouillon

1 tsp Chinese five-spice powder

2 tsp Chinese rice wine or dry sherry

1 tsp cornstarch

2 tsp water

1 tsp sesame oil

NUTRITION

Calories *162*; Sugars *2 g*; Protein *20 g*; Carbohydrate *3 g*; Fat *7 g*; Saturates *2 g*

⊕⊕⊕ moderate

🕐 10 mins

🕐 25 mins

🍳 **COOK'S TIP**

Omit the chile for a milder dish, or seed the chile before adding it to remove some of the heat.

Use fresh mangoes in this recipe for terrific flavor and color. If they are unavailable, use canned mangoes and rinse them before use.

Duck *with* Mangoes

SERVES 4

2 ripe mangoes, peeled, pitted and cut into strips
1¼ cups chicken bouillon
2 garlic cloves, crushed
1 tsp grated fresh gingerroot
2 large skinless duck breasts, about 8 oz/225 g each
3 tbsp vegetable oil
1 tsp rice wine vinegar
1 tsp light soy sauce
1 leek, cut into ribbons
chopped fresh parsley, to garnish

NUTRITION

Calories 235; Sugars 6 g; Protein 23 g; Carbohydrate 6 g; Fat 14 g; Saturates 2 g

moderate

10 mins

30 mins

1 Put half of the mango strips and the chicken bouillon in a food processor and process until smooth. Alternatively, press half of the mangoes through a fine strainer and mix with the bouillon.

2 Rub the garlic and ginger over the duck. Heat the vegetable oil in a preheated wok or large, heavy-based skillet and cook the duck breasts, turning, until seared. Reserve the oil in the wok and remove the duck using a slotted spoon.

3 Place the duck on a rack set over a roasting pan and cook in a preheated oven, 425°F/220°C for 20 minutes, until the duck is cooked through.

4 Meanwhile, place the mango and bouillon mixture in a pan and add the rice wine vinegar and light soy sauce.

5 Bring the mixture in the pan to a boil and cook over a high heat, stirring, until reduced by half.

6 Heat the oil reserved in the wok and cook the leek and remaining mango for 1 minute. Remove from the wok, transfer to a serving dish and keep warm until required.

7 Slice the cooked duck breasts and arrange on top of the leek and mango mixture. Pour the sauce over the duck, garnish with parsley and serve.

Duck is a strongly flavored meat, which benefits from the added citrus peel to counteract this rich taste.

Duck *with* Leek *and* Cabbage

1 Heat a preheated wok or large, heavy-based skillet and dry-cook the duck breasts, with the skin on, for about 5 minutes on each side (you may need to do this in 2 batches).

2 Remove the duck breasts from the wok using a slotted spoon and transfer to a clean board. Using a sharp knife, cut the duck breasts into thin slices.

3 Remove all but 1 tablespoon of the fat from the duck left in the wok; discard the rest.

4 Add the green cabbage, leeks, and orange zest to the wok and cook for about 5 minutes, or until the vegetables have softened.

5 Return the duck to the wok and heat through for 2–3 minutes.

6 Drizzle the oyster sauce over the mixture in the wok, toss well until all the ingredients are combined and then heat through.

7 Scatter the stir-fry with toasted sesame seeds, transfer to a warm serving dish and serve hot.

COOK'S TIP

Use Napa cabbage for a lighter, sweeter flavor instead of the green cabbage, if you prefer.

SERVES 4

4 duck breasts, about 8 oz/225 g each
12 oz/350 g green cabbage, shredded thinly
8 oz/225 g leeks, sliced
finely grated zest of 1 orange
6 tbsp oyster sauce
1 tsp toasted sesame seeds, to serve

NUTRITION

Calories 140; Sugars 3 g; Protein 3 g; Carbohydrate 20 g; Fat 17 g; Saturates 1 g

 moderate

15 mins

20 mins

The pineapple and plum sauce add a sweetness and fruity flavor to this colorful dish, which also blends well with the duck.

Fruity Duck Stir-Fry

SERVES 4

1 tsp Chinese five-spice powder
1 tbsp cornstarch
4 skinless duck breasts, sliced thinly
1 tbsp chili oil
8 oz/225 g pearl onions, peeled
2 garlic cloves, crushed
3½ oz/100 g baby corn cobs
1¼ cups canned pineapple chunks, drained
6 scallions, sliced
1 cup beansprouts
2 tbsp plum sauce

1 Mix together the Chinese five-spice powder and the cornstarch. Toss the duck in the mixture until well coated.

2 Heat the oil in a preheated wok or large, heavy-based skillet. Cook the duck for 10 minutes, or until just beginning to crisp around the edges. Remove from the wok and set aside.

3 Add the onions and garlic to the wok and cook for 5 minutes, or until softened. Add the baby corn cobs and cook for another 5 minutes. Add the pineapple, scallions, and beansprouts and cook for 3–4 minutes. Stir in the plum sauce.

4 Return the cooked duck to the wok and toss until well mixed and heated through. Transfer to warm serving dishes and serve hot.

NUTRITION

Calories *241*; Sugars *7 g*; Protein *26 g*;
Carbohydrate *16 g*; Fat *8 g*; Saturates *2 g*

easy

5 mins

25 mins

🍳 **COOK'S TIP**

Buy pineapple chunks in natural juice rather than syrup for a fresher flavor. If you can only obtain pineapple in syrup, rinse it in cold water and drain thoroughly before using.

Satay sauce is easy to make and is one of the best known and loved sauces in Asian cooking. It is perfect with beef, chicken, or pork.

Pork Satay Stir-Fry

1 Heat the oil in a preheated wok or large, heavy-based skillet. Add the pork, onion, and garlic and cook for 5 minutes, or until the pork is cooked through.

2 Add the carrots, yellow bell pepper, snow peas and asparagus to the wok, and cook for 5 minutes.

3 To make the satay sauce, place the peanut butter, coconut milk, chili flakes, garlic, and tomato paste in a small pan and heat gently, stirring, until well combined. Be careful not to let the sauce stick to the bottom of the pan.

4 Transfer the stir-fry to warm serving plates. Spoon the satay sauce over the stir-fry and scatter with chopped peanuts. Serve immediately.

SERVES 4

2 tbsp sunflower oil
12 oz/350 g pork tenderloin, sliced thinly
1 onion, sliced
2 garlic cloves, crushed
2 small carrots, cut into thin sticks
1 yellow bell pepper, seeded and sliced
5$\frac{1}{2}$ oz/150 g snow peas
2$\frac{3}{4}$ oz/75 g fine asparagus
chopped salted peanuts, to serve

satay sauce
6 tbsp crunchy peanut butter
6 tbsp coconut milk
1 tsp dried chili flakes
1 garlic clove, crushed
1 tsp tomato paste

NUTRITION
Calories *506*; Sugars *11 g*; Protein *31 g*;
Carbohydrate *15 g*; Fat *36 g*; Saturates *8 g*

moderate
10 mins
15 mins

COOK'S TIP

Cook the sauce just before serving as it tends to thicken very quickly and will not be spoonable if you prepare it too far in advance.

Pork is coated in a spicy mixture before being cooked until crisp and then stirred into a delicious egg rice for a very filling meal.

Spicy Pork *and* Rice

SERVES 4

1¼ cups long-grain white rice
2½ cups cold water
2 tsp Chinese five-spice powder
4 tbsp cornstarch
3 large eggs, beaten (one kept separate)
2 tbsp brown sugar
12 oz/350 g pork tenderloin, sliced thinly
2 tbsp sunflower oil
1 onion, diced
2 garlic cloves, crushed
1 large carrot, diced
1 red bell pepper, seeded and diced
¾ cup frozen peas
1 tbsp butter
salt and pepper

NUTRITION

Calories *599*; Sugars *11 g*; Protein *30 g*;
Carbohydrate *76 g*; Fat *22 g*; Saturates *7 g*

✪✪✪✪ challenging

🕐 10 mins

🕐 35 mins

1 Rinse the rice under cold running water. Place the rice in a large pan, add the cold water and a pinch of salt. Bring to a boil, cover, then reduce the heat and let simmer for about 9 minutes, or until all of the liquid has been absorbed and the rice is tender. Leave to cool.

2 Whisk together the Chinese five-spice powder, cornstarch, 1 egg, and the brown sugar. Toss the pork in the mixture until well coated.

3 Heat the sunflower oil in a preheated wok or large, heavy-based skillet. Add the pork and cook over a high heat until it is cooked through and crispy. Remove the pork from the wok with a slotted spoon and set aside until required.

4 Add the onion, garlic, carrot, red bell pepper, and peas to the wok and cook for 5 minutes.

5 Return the pork to the wok with the cooked rice and cook for 5 minutes.

6 Heat the butter in a skillet. Add the remaining eggs and cook until set. Turn out on to a clean board and thinly slice. Toss the strips of egg into the rice mixture and serve immediately.

These small meatballs are packed with flavor and cooked in a tangy tomato sauce for a delicious meal.

Spicy Pork Balls

1 Place the ground pork in a large mixing bowl. Add the shallots, garlic, cumin seeds, chili powder, bread crumbs, and beaten egg, and mix together well.

2 Form the mixture into balls between the palms of your hands.

3 Heat the oil in a preheated wok or large, heavy-based skillet. Add the pork balls and cook, in batches, over a high heat for about 5 minutes, or until seared on all sides. Remove from the wok and drain on paper towels.

4 Add the tomatoes, soy sauce, and water chestnuts to the wok and bring to a boil. Return the pork balls to the wok, stirring them carefully to coat them in the sauce, reduce the heat, and let simmer for 15 minutes.

5 Scatter with chopped fresh cilantro and serve hot.

SERVES 4

1 lb/450 g ground pork
2 shallots, chopped finely
2 garlic cloves, crushed
1 tsp cumin seeds
½ tsp chili powder
½ cup fresh whole-wheat bread crumbs
1 egg, beaten
2 tbsp sunflower oil
14 oz/400 g canned chopped tomatoes, flavored with chile
2 tbsp soy sauce
7 oz/200 g canned water chestnuts, drained
3 tbsp chopped fresh cilantro

NUTRITION
Calories 299; Sugars 3 g; Protein 28 g; Carbohydrate 14 g; Fat 15 g; Saturates 4 g

★★★★ challenging
🕐 10 mins
🕐 40 mins

🍳 **COOK'S TIP**

Add a few teaspoons of chili sauce to a tin of chopped tomatoes, if you can't find the flavored variety.

In this classic Chinese dish, tender pork is cooked and served in a fruity sauce. This dish is perfect served with plain rice.

Sweet *and* Sour Pork

SERVES 4

2 tbsp sunflower oil
1 lb/450 g pork tenderloin, cut into bite-size pieces
1 red onion, cut into thin wedges
2 garlic cloves, crushed
3 carrots, cut into thin sticks
8 oz/225 g zucchini, cut into thin sticks
1 red bell pepper, seeded and sliced
3½ oz/100 g baby corn cobs
3½ oz/100 g white mushrooms, halved
1¼ cups fresh cubed pineapple
1 cup beansprouts
⅔ cup pineapple juice
1 tbsp cornstarch
2 tbsp soy sauce
3 tbsp tomato catsup
1 tbsp white wine vinegar
1 tbsp clear honey

1 Heat the sunflower oil in a preheated wok or large, heavy-based skillet. Add the pork to the wok and cook for 10 minutes, or until the pork is completely cooked through and beginning to turn crispy at the edges.

2 Add the onion, garlic, carrots, zucchini, red bell pepper, baby corn cobs, and mushrooms to the wok, and cook for a further 5 minutes.

3 Add the pineapple and beansprouts to the wok and cook for 2 minutes.

4 Mix together the pineapple juice, cornstarch, soy sauce, tomato catsup, white wine vinegar, and honey.

5 Pour the sweet and sour mixture into the wok and cook over a high heat, tossing frequently, until the juices have thickened. Transfer the pork to serving bowls and serve hot.

NUTRITION
Calories 357; Sugars 25 g; Protein 28 g;
Carbohydrate 30 g; Fat 14 g; Saturates 4 g

⭐⭐⭐ moderate
🕐 10 mins
🕐 20 mins

COOK'S TIP

If you prefer a crisper coating, toss the pork in a mixture of cornstarch and egg white and deep fry in the wok in step 2.

Pork and daikon are a perfect combination, especially with the added heat of the sweet chili sauce. Daikon has a similar flavor to radish.

Pork *with* Daikon

1 Heat 2 tablespoons of the vegetable oil in a preheated wok or large, heavy-based skillet.

2 Add the pork to the wok and cook for about 5 minutes.

3 Add the remaining vegetable oil to the wok. Add the eggplant to the wok with the garlic and cook for another 5 minutes.

4 Add the daikon to the wok and cook for about 2 minutes.

5 Stir the soy sauce and sweet chili sauce into the mixture in the wok and cook until heated through.

6 Transfer the pork and daikon to warm serving bowls and serve immediately with boiled rice or noodles.

SERVES 4

4 tbsp vegetable oil
1 lb/450 g pork tenderloin, cut into bite-size pieces
1 eggplant, diced
8 oz/225 g daikon, sliced
2 garlic cloves, crushed
3 tbsp soy sauce
2 tbsp sweet chili sauce
boiled rice or noodles, to serve

NUTRITION
Calories *280*; Sugars *1 g*; Protein *25 g*; Carbohydrate *2 g*; Fat *19 g*; Saturates *4 g*

⭐⭐⭐   moderate

🕐   10 mins

🕐   15 mins

This is a very simple dish, which lends itself to almost any combination of vegetables that you have to hand.

Pork *with* Vegetables

SERVES 4

2 tbsp vegetable oil

2 garlic cloves, crushed

½-inch/1-cm piece of fresh gingerroot, cut into slivers

12 oz/350 g pork tenderloin, cut into thin slices

1 carrot, cut into thin strips

1 red bell pepper, seeded and diced

1 fennel bulb, sliced

1 oz/25 g canned water chestnuts, drained and halved

¾ cup beansprouts

2 tbsp Chinese rice wine

1¼ cups pork or chicken bouillon

pinch of dark brown sugar

1 tsp cornstarch

2 tsp water

1 Heat the oil in a preheated wok or large, heavy-based skillet. Add the garlic, ginger, and pork, and cook for 1–2 minutes, until the meat is seared.

2 Add the carrot, red bell pepper, fennel, and water chestnuts to the wok, and cook for about 2–3 minutes.

3 Add the beansprouts and cook for 1 minute. Remove the pork and vegetables from the wok and keep warm.

4 Add the Chinese rice wine, pork bouillon, and sugar to the wok. Blend the cornstarch to a smooth paste with the water and stir it into the sauce. Bring to a boil, stirring constantly, until thickened and clear.

5 Return the meat and vegetables to the wok and cook for 1–2 minutes, until heated through and coated with the sauce. Serve immediately.

NUTRITION

Calories 216; Sugars 3 g; Protein 19 g; Carbohydrate 5 g; Fat 12 g; Saturates 3 g

moderate

5 mins

15 mins

(icon) COOK'S TIP

If you have difficulty finding Chinese rice wine, use dry sherry instead .

Plum sauce is often used in Chinese cooking with duck or dark meat to balance the flavor of the meat.

Pork *with* Plums

1 Combine the cornstarch, soy sauce, Chinese rice wine, sugar, and cinnamon.

2 Place the pork in a shallow dish and pour the cornstarch mixture over it. Toss the meat in the marinade until it is completely coated. Cover and let marinate in the refrigerator for at least 30 minutes. Remove the pork from the dish with a slotted spoon, reserving the marinade.

3 Heat the oil in a preheated wok or large, heavy-based skillet. Add the pork and cook for 3–4 minutes, until a light golden color.

4 Stir in the garlic, scallions, plum sauce, Peking sauce, water, and chili sauce. Bring the sauce to a boil. Reduce the heat, cover, and let simmer for 8–10 minutes, or until the pork is cooked through and tender.

5 Stir in the reserved marinade and cook, stirring, for about 5 minutes.

6 Transfer the pork stir-fry to a warm serving dish and garnish with fried plum quarters and scallions. Serve immediately.

SERVES 4

1 tbsp cornstarch
2 tbsp light soy sauce
2 tbsp Chinese rice wine
4 tsp light brown sugar
pinch of ground cinnamon
1 lb/450 g pork tenderloin, sliced thinly
5 tsp vegetable oil
2 garlic cloves, crushed
2 scallions, chopped
4 tbsp plum sauce
1 tbsp Peking sauce
$^2/_3$ cup water
dash of chili sauce

to garnish
fried plum quarters
sliced scallions

NUTRITION
Calories *140*; Sugars *3 g*; Protein *3 g*;
Carbohydrate *20 g*; Fat *17 g*; Saturates *1 g*

★★★ moderate
🕐 40 mins
🕐 20 mins

Small pieces of pork are coated in a light batter and deep-fried in this recipe— they are delicious dipped in a soy and honey sauce.

Deep-Fried Pork Fritters

SERVES 4

2 tbsp peanut oil
1 lb/450 g pork tenderloin, cut into 1-inch/2.5-cm cubes
scant 1½ cups all-purpose flour
2 tsp baking powder
1 egg, beaten
scant 1 cup milk
pinch of chili powder
vegetable oil, for deep-frying
fresh chives, to garnish

sauce
2 tbsp dark soy sauce
3 tbsp clear honey
1 tbsp rice wine vinegar
1 tbsp tomato paste
1 tbsp snipped fresh chives

NUTRITION
Calories 528; Sugars 12 g; Protein 32 g;
Carbohydrate 52 g; Fat 22 g; Saturates 6 g

✪✪✪ moderate
🕐 15 mins
🕐 20 mins

1 Heat the peanut oil in a preheated wok or large, heavy-based skillet. Add the pork to the wok and cook for 2–3 minutes, until seared.

2 Remove the pork with a slotted spoon and set aside until required.

3 Strain the flour and baking powder into a mixing bowl and make a well in the center. Gradually beat in the egg, milk, and chili powder to make a thick, smooth batter.

4 Heat the oil for deep-frying in a wok or large heavy-based pan until almost smoking, then reduce the heat slightly.

5 Toss the pork pieces in the batter to coat thoroughly. Add the pork to the wok and deep-fry until golden brown and cooked through. Remove with a slotted spoon and drain well on paper towels.

6 Meanwhile, make the sauce. Mix together all the ingredients and spoon into a small serving bowl.

7 Transfer the pork fritters to serving dishes, garnish with chives and serve with the sauce.

This classic dish features lamb marinated in chili and coconut and threaded on to wooden skewers.

Lamb *with* Satay Sauce

1 Mix together the curry paste, coconut milk, garlic, chili powder, and cumin in a bowl. Pour the marinade over the lamb, toss well, cover, and marinate in the refrigerator for 30 minutes.

2 To make the satay sauce, heat the oil in a preheated wok or large, heavy-based skillet. Add the onion and cook for 5 minutes, then reduce the heat and cook for another 5 minutes.

3 Stir in the peanut butter, tomato paste, lime juice, and water.

4 Thread the lamb on to wooden skewers, reserving the marinade.

5 Broil the lamb skewers under a hot broiler for 6–8 minutes, turning once.

6 Add the reserved marinade to the sauce in the wok, bring to a boil and cook for 5 minutes. Serve the lamb skewers with the satay sauce.

SERVES 4

1 tbsp mild curry paste
2/3 cup coconut milk
2 garlic cloves, crushed
1/2 tsp chili powder
1/2 tsp ground cumin
1 lb/450 g lamb loin fillet, sliced thinly

satay sauce
1 tbsp corn oil
1 onion, diced
6 tbsp crunchy peanut butter
1 tsp tomato paste
1 tsp fresh lime juice
generous 1/3 cup cold water

NUTRITION
Calories *501*; Sugars *6 g*; Protein *34 g*; Carbohydrate *9 g*; Fat *37 g*; Saturates *10 g*

⭐⭐⭐   moderate

🕐   35 mins

🕐   25 mins

👨‍🍳 **COOK'S TIP**

Soak the wooden skewers in cold water for 30 minutes before threading the lamb and broiling to prevent them from burning.

Red onions complement the colors of the bell peppers in this dish— they taste good, too.

Lamb *with* Black Bean Sauce

SERVES 4

1 egg white, beaten lightly

4 tbsp cornstarch

1 tsp Chinese five-spice powder

1 lb/450 g lamb neck fillet or boneless leg of lamb, cut into thin strips

3 tbsp sunflower oil

1 red onion, sliced

1 red bell pepper, seeded and sliced

1 green bell pepper, seeded and sliced

1 yellow or orange bell pepper, seeded and sliced

5 tbsp black bean sauce

boiled rice or noodles, to serve

1 Mix together the egg white, cornstarch, and Chinese five-spice powder. Toss the lamb strips in the mixture until evenly coated.

2 Heat the oil in a preheated wok or large, heavy-based skillet and cook the lamb over a high heat for 5 minutes, or until it becomes crispy around the edges.

3 Add the onion and red, green, and yellow bell peppers to the wok and cook for 5–6 minutes, or until the vegetables have softened.

4 Stir the black bean sauce into the mixture in the wok and heat through.

5 Transfer the lamb and sauce to warm serving plates and serve hot with rice or noodles.

NUTRITION

Calories *328*; Sugars *5 g*; Protein *26 g*; Carbohydrate *12 g*; Fat *20 g*; Saturates *6 g*

easy

10 mins

15 mins

👨‍🍳 COOK'S TIP

Take care when frying the lamb as the cornstarch mixture may cause it to stick to the wok. Move the lamb around the wok constantly while cooking.

This really is a speedy dish, lamb leg steaks being perfect for the short cooking time.

Oyster Sauce Lamb

1 Sprinkle the ground Szechuan peppercorns over the lamb and toss together until well combined.

2 Heat the peanut oil in a preheated wok or large, heavy-based skillet.

3 Add the lamb to the wok and cook for about 5 minutes.

4 Add the garlic and scallions to the wok, together with the dark soy sauce, and cook for 2 minutes.

5 Add the oyster sauce and Napa cabbage and cook for another 2 minutes, or until the cabbage has wilted and the juices are bubbling.

6 Transfer the stir-fry to warm serving bowls and serve hot with shrimp crackers, if liked.

SERVES 4

1 tsp ground Szechuan peppercorns
1 lb/450 g lamb leg steaks, sliced thinly
1 tbsp peanut oil
2 garlic cloves, crushed
8 scallions, sliced
2 tbsp dark soy sauce
6 tbsp oyster sauce
6 oz/175 g Napa cabbage, shredded
shrimp crackers, to serve (optional)

NUTRITION
Calories *243*; Sugars *0.4 g*; Protein *26 g*;
Carbohydrate *3 g*; Fat *14 g*; Saturates *5 g*

⭐ very easy

🕐 5 mins

🕐 10 mins

COOK'S TIP

Oyster sauce is made from oysters which are cooked in brine and soy sauce. Sold in bottles, it will keep in the refrigerator for up to a month.

The long marinating time allows the garlic to penetrate the meat, creating a much more flavorful dish.

Garlic Lamb *with* Soy Sauce

SERVES 4

2 garlic cloves, sliced
1 lb/450 g lamb loin fillet, slashed
2 tbsp peanut oil
3 tbsp dry sherry or Chinese rice wine
3 tbsp dark soy sauce
1 tsp cornstarch
2 tbsp cold water
2 tbsp butter, cut into small pieces

1 Push the slices of garlic into the slits in the lamb. Place the garlic-infused lamb in a shallow dish.

2 In a small bowl, mix together 1 tablespoon each of the peanut oil, dry sherry, and dark soy sauce. Drizzle this mixture over the lamb, cover with plastic wrap and marinate in the refrigerator for at least 1 hour, or preferably overnight.

3 Using a sharp knife or meat cleaver, thinly slice the marinated lamb.

4 Heat the remaining oil in a preheated wok or large, heavy-based skillet. Add the marinated lamb and cook for 5 minutes.

5 Add the marinade juices and the remaining sherry, and soy sauce to the wok and allow the juices to bubble for 5 minutes.

6 Blend the cornstarch to a smooth paste with the cold water. Add the cornstarch mixture to the wok and cook, stirring occasionally, until the juices start to thicken and clear.

7 Add the butter to the wok and stir until the butter melts. Transfer the lamb to serving dishes and serve immediately.

NUTRITION
Calories *309*; Sugars *0.2 g*; Protein *25 g*;
Carbohydrate *3 g*; Fat *21 g*; Saturates *9 g*

easy

1hr 15 mins

15 mins

Peanut oil is used here for flavor—it is a popular oil for stir-fries because it has a high smoking point.

Lamb *with* Lime Leaves

1 Heat the peanut oil in a preheated wok or large, heavy-based skillet.

2 Add the garlic, shallots, lemongrass, lime leaves, tamarind paste, palm sugar, and chiles to the wok and cook for about 2 minutes.

3 Add the lamb and cook for about 5 minutes, tossing well so that it is evenly coated in the spice mixture.

4 Pour the coconut milk into the wok and bring to a boil. Reduce the heat and let simmer for 20 minutes.

5 Add the tomatoes and cilantro to the wok and let simmer for 5 minutes. Transfer to serving plates and serve hot with fragrant rice.

SERVES 4

2 tbsp peanut oil
2 garlic cloves, crushed
4 shallots, chopped
2 lemongrass stems, sliced
6 lime leaves
1 tbsp tamarind paste
2 tbsp palm sugar
2 fresh red chiles, seeded and chopped finely
1 lb/450 g lean leg of lamb or loin fillet, cut into bite-size pieces
2½ cups coconut milk
6 oz/175 g cherry tomatoes, halved
1 tbsp chopped fresh cilantro
boiled fragrant rice, to serve

NUTRITION
Calories *302*; Sugars *15 g*; Protein *24 g*; Carbohydrate *17 g*; Fat *16 g*; Saturates *6 g*

⊛⊛⊛ moderate

◔ 10 mins

◕ 35 mins

🍳 **COOK'S TIP**

When buying fresh cilantro, look for bright green, unwilted leaves. To store it, wash and dry the leaves, leaving them on the stem. Wrap the leaves in damp paper towels and keep them in a plastic bag in the refrigerator.

These small meatballs are made with ground lamb and flavored with chili, garlic, parsley, and Chinese curry powder.

Lamb Meatballs

SERVES 4

1 lb/450 g ground lamb
3 garlic cloves, crushed
2 scallions, chopped finely
1/2 tsp chili powder
1 tsp Chinese curry powder
1 tbsp chopped fresh parsley
1/2 cup fresh white bread crumbs
1 egg, beaten
3 tbsp vegetable oil
4 1/2 oz/125 g Napa cabbage, shredded
1 leek, sliced
1 tbsp cornstarch
2 tbsp water
1 1/4 cups lamb bouillon
1 tbsp dark soy sauce
shredded leek, to garnish

1 Mix together the lamb, garlic, scallions, chili powder, Chinese curry powder, parsley, and bread crumbs in a bowl. Work the egg into the mixture, bringing it together to form a firm mixture. Roll into 16 small, even-sized balls.

2 Heat the oil in a preheated wok or large, heavy-based skillet. Add the Napa cabbage and leek and cook for 1 minute. Remove from the wok with a slotted spoon and set aside.

3 Add the meatballs to the wok and cook in batches, turning gently, for 3–4 minutes, or until golden brown.

4 Mix the cornstarch and water together to form a smooth paste and set aside. Pour the lamb bouillon and soy sauce into the wok and cook for 2–3 minutes. Stir in the cornstarch paste. Bring to a boil and cook, stirring constantly, until the sauce has thickened and cleared.

5 Return the Napa cabbage and leek to the wok and cook for 1 minute, until heated through. Arrange the Napa cabbage and leek on a warm serving dish, top with the meatballs, then garnish with the shredded leek and serve.

NUTRITION
Calories *320*; Sugars *1 g*; Protein *28 g*;
Carbohydrate *8 g*; Fat *20 g*; Saturates *6 g*

✪✪✪   moderate

🕐   5 mins

🕐   20 mins

This richly spiced curry uses the typically red-hot chile flavor of red curry paste, which gives it a warm, russet-red color.

Red Lamb Curry

1 Heat the oil in a preheated wok or large, heavy-based skillet over a high heat and cook the onion and garlic for 2–3 minute, until softened. Add the meat and cook the mixture quickly until lightly browned.

2 Stir in the red curry paste and cook for a few seconds, then add the coconut milk and sugar and bring to a boil. Reduce the heat and let simmer for 15 minutes, stirring occasionally.

3 Stir in the red bell pepper, lamb bouillon, fish sauce, and lime juice, cover and let simmer for another 15 minutes, or until the meat is tender.

4 Add the water chestnuts, cilantro, and basil, season with salt and pepper to taste. Serve with jasmine rice, garnished with fresh basil leaves.

SERVES 4

2 tbsp vegetable oil
1 large onion, sliced
2 garlic cloves, crushed
1 lb 2 oz/500 g boneless lean leg of lamb, cut into 1¼-inch/3-cm cubes
2 tbsp Thai red curry paste
⅔ cup coconut milk
1 tbsp light brown sugar
1 large red bell pepper, seeded and sliced
½ cup lamb or beef bouillon
1 tbsp fish sauce
2 tbsp lime juice
8 oz/225 g canned water chestnuts, drained
2 tbsp chopped fresh cilantro
2 tbsp chopped fresh basil
salt and pepper
boiled jasmine rice, to serve
fresh basil leaves, to garnish

NUTRITION

Calories *363*; Sugars *11 g*; Protein *29 g*; Carbohydrate *21 g*; Fat *19 g*; Saturates *6 g*

  moderate

5 mins

40 mins

🍳 COOK'S TIP

This curry can also be made with other lean red meats. Try replacing the lamb with trimmed duck breasts or pieces of lean braising beef.

This is a very simple, yet delicious dish, in which lean pieces of lamb are cooked in a sweet soy sauce and then sprinkled with sesame seeds.

Sesame Lamb Stir-Fry

SERVES 4

2 tbsp peanut oil
1 lb/450 g boneless lean lamb, cut into thin strips
2 leeks, sliced
1 carrot, cut into matchsticks
2 garlic cloves, crushed
⅓ cup lamb or vegetable bouillon
2 tsp light brown sugar
1 tbsp dark soy sauce
4½ tsp sesame seeds

1 Heat the peanut oil in a preheated wok or large, heavy-based skillet until it is really hot.

2 Add the lamb and cook for 2–3 minutes. Remove the lamb from the wok with a slotted spoon and set aside until required.

3 Add the leeks, carrot, and garlic to the wok and cook for 1–2 minutes. Remove the vegetables from the wok with a slotted spoon and set aside.

4 Drain any remaining oil from the wok. Place the lamb bouillon, light brown sugar, and dark soy sauce in the wok and add the lamb. Cook, stirring constantly, for 2–3 minutes, until the lamb is coated in the mixture.

5 Sprinkle the sesame seeds over the top, turning the lamb to coat.

6 Spoon the leek, carrot, and garlic mixture on to a warm serving dish and top with the lamb. Serve immediately.

NUTRITION
Calories 276; Sugars 4 g; Protein 25 g;
Carbohydrate 5 g; Fat 18 g; Saturates 6 g

easy

5 mins

10 mins

🍳 **COOK'S TIP**

Be careful not to burn the sugar in the wok when coating the meat, otherwise the flavor of the dish will be spoiled.

In this recipe, beef is marinated in a spicy chili marinade for a really rich flavor.

Spicy Beef

1 Mix together the garlic, star anise, and dark soy sauce in a bowl.

2 Pour the spice mixture over the steak, turning it to coat thoroughly, cover and marinate in the refrigerator for at least 1 hour.

3 To make the sauce, heat the oil in a preheated wok or large, heavy-based skillet. Reduce the heat and cook the scallions for 1–2 minutes.

4 Remove the scallions from the wok with a slotted spoon, drain on paper towels and set aside until required.

5 Add the beef to the wok with the marinade, and cook for 3–4 minutes. Return the scallions to the wok and add the soy sauce, sherry, chili sauce, and two-thirds of the water.

6 Blend the cornstarch with the remaining water and stir it into the wok. Bring to a boil, stirring, until the sauce has thickened and cleared.

7 Transfer to a warm serving dish and serve immediately.

SERVES **4**

2 garlic cloves, crushed
1 tsp ground star anise
1 tbsp dark soy sauce
8 oz/225 g beef, cut into thin strips

sauce
2 tbsp vegetable oil
1 bunch scallions, halved lengthwise
1 tbsp dark soy sauce
1 tbsp dry sherry
$\frac{1}{4}$ tsp chili sauce
$\frac{2}{3}$ cup water
2 tsp cornstarch

NUTRITION
Calories *246*; Sugars *2 g*; Protein *21 g*;
Carbohydrate *10 g*; Fat *13 g*; Saturates *3 g*

easy

1 hr 15 mins

20 mins

Beef is perfect for stir-fries as it is so tender and lends itself to quick cooking.

Stir-Fried Beef *and* Vegetables

SERVES 4

2 tbsp sunflower oil
12 oz/350 g beef fillet, sliced
1 red onion, sliced
2 carrots, sliced thinly
1 red bell pepper, seeded and sliced
6 oz/175 g zucchini, sliced diagonally
1 small head Napa cabbage, shredded
1½ cups beansprouts
8 oz/225 g canned bamboo shoots, drained
1½ cups cashews, toasted

sauce

3 tbsp medium sherry
3 tbsp light soy sauce
1 tsp ground ginger
1 garlic clove, crushed
1 tsp cornstarch
1 tbsp tomato paste

1 Heat the sunflower oil in a preheated wok or large, heavy-based skillet. Add the beef and red onion to the wok and cook for about 4–5 minutes, or until the onion has softened and the meat begins to brown.

2 Add the carrots, bell pepper, and zucchini to the wok and cook the mixture for 5 minutes.

3 Toss in the Napa cabbage, beansprouts, and bamboo shoots and heat through for 2–3 minutes, or until the leaves are just beginning to wilt.

4 Scatter the cashews over the stir-fry and toss well to mix.

5 To make the sauce, mix together all the ingredients until well combined.

6 Pour the sauce over the stir-fry and toss to mix. Allow the sauce to bubble for 2–3 minutes, or until the juices thicken.

7 Transfer to warm serving bowls and serve at once.

NUTRITION
Calories 521; Sugars 7 g; Protein 31 g;
Carbohydrate 18 g; Fat 35 g; Saturates 8 g

✪✪✪   moderate
         10 mins
         20 mins

Tender beef, marinated in a soy and tomato sauce, is cooked with crisp bamboo shoots and snow peas in this simple recipe.

Beef *with* Bamboo Shoots

1 Place the beef in a nonmetallic dish with the dark soy sauce, tomato catsup, garlic, lemon juice, and ground coriander. Mix well to coat the meat in the marinade, cover, and marinate in the refrigerator for at least 1 hour.

2 Heat the vegetable oil in a preheated wok or large, heavy-based skillet. Add the meat to the wok and cook for 2–4 minutes (depending on how well cooked you like your meat), or until cooked through.

3 Add the snow peas and bamboo shoots to the mixture in the wok and cook over a high heat, tossing frequently, for another 5 minutes.

4 Drizzle with the sesame oil and toss well to combine. Transfer to serving dishes and serve hot.

SERVES 4

12 oz/350 g rump steak, sliced thinly
3 tbsp dark soy sauce
1 tbsp tomato catsup
2 garlic cloves, crushed
1 tbsp fresh lemon juice
1 tsp ground coriander
2 tbsp vegetable oil
6 oz/175 g snow peas
7 oz/200 g canned bamboo shoots, drained
1 tsp sesame oil

NUTRITION
Calories 275; Sugars 3 g; Protein 21 g;
Carbohydrate 6 g; Fat 19 g; Saturates 6 g

easy

1 hr 15 mins

10 mins

🧑‍🍳 **COOK'S TIP**

Leave the meat to marinate for at least 1 hour in order for the flavors to penetrate and increase the tenderness of the meat.

It is unnecessary to use expensive cuts of beef steak for this recipe: the meat will be tender as it is cut into small, thin slices and marinated.

Beef *and* Black Bean Sauce

SERVES 4

about 1¼ cups vegetable oil
9–10½ oz/250–300 g beef steak, such as rump, cut into thin strips
1 scallion, cut into short sections
a few small slices of fresh gingerroot
1–2 small fresh green or red chiles, seeded and sliced
1 small onion, chopped
1 small green bell pepper, seeded and diced
2 tbsp black bean sauce

marinade
½ tsp baking soda or baking powder
½ tsp sugar
1 tbsp light soy sauce
2 tsp Chinese rice wine or dry sherry
2 tsp cornstarch
2 tsp sesame oil

NUTRITION

Calories *392*; Sugars *2 g*; Protein *13 g*;
Carbohydrate *3 g*; Fat *36 g*; Saturates *7 g*

    easy

🕐   3hrs 15 mins

🕐   5 mins

1 To make the marinade, mix together all the ingredients in a shallow dish. Add the beef, turn to coat and marinate in the refrigerator for at least 2–3 hours.

2 Heat the vegetable oil in a preheated wok or large, heavy-based skillet. Add the beef and cook for about 1 minute, or until seared. Remove the beef with a slotted spoon and drain on paper towels. Keep warm and set aside.

3 Pour all but 1 tablespoon of the oil from the wok. Add the scallion, ginger, chiles, onion, and green bell pepper and cook for about 1 minute.

4 Add the black bean sauce and stir until smooth. Return the beef to the wok, stir well and cook for another minute. Transfer the stir-fry to a warm serving dish and serve hot.

🍳 COOK'S TIP

You could use chicken, turkey, lean pork, or even strips of venison instead of beef in this recipe.

Soy sauce and sesame seeds are classic ingredients in Chinese cooking. Use a dark soy sauce for a fuller flavor and richness.

Soy *and* Sesame Beef

1 Heat a wok or large, heavy-based skillet until it is very hot.

2 Add the sesame seeds to the wok and dry-cook, stirring, for 1–2 minutes, or until they just begin to brown. Remove the sesame seeds from the wok and set aside until required.

3 Heat the vegetable oil in the wok. Add the beef and cook for 2–3 minutes, or until seared on all sides.

4 Add the green bell pepper and garlic to the wok and continue to cook for 2 minutes.

5 Add the dry sherry and soy sauce to the wok with the scallions. Allow the mixture in the wok to bubble, stirring occasionally, for about 1 minute, but do not let the mixture burn.

6 Transfer the beef stir-fry to warm serving bowls and scatter with the dry-cooked sesame seeds. Serve hot with egg noodles.

SERVES 4

2 tbsp sesame seeds
2 tbsp vegetable oil
1 lb/450 g beef fillet, sliced thinly
1 green bell pepper, seeded and sliced thinly
4 garlic cloves, crushed
2 tbsp dry sherry
4 tbsp soy sauce
6 scallions, sliced
boiled egg noodles, to serve

COOK'S TIP

You can spread the sesame seeds out on a baking sheet and toast them under a preheated grill until browned all over, if you prefer.

NUTRITION
Calories 324; Sugars 2 g; Protein 25 g; Carbohydrate 3 g; Fat 22 g; Saturates 6 g

easy

5 mins

10 mins

A delicately flavored stir-fry, which is infused with lemongrass and ginger. Colorful bell peppers help to complete the dish.

Beef *with* Lemongrass

SERVES 4

2 tbsp vegetable oil
1 garlic clove, chopped finely
1 lb 2 oz/500 g beef fillet, cut into long, thin strips across the grain
1 lemongrass stem, shredded finely
2 tsp chopped finely fresh gingerroot
1 red bell pepper, seeded and thickly sliced
1 green bell pepper, seeded and thickly sliced
1 onion, sliced thickly
2 tbsp lime juice
salt and pepper
boiled noodles or rice, to serve

1 Heat the oil in a preheated wok or large, heavy-based skillet over a high heat. Add the garlic and cook for 1 minute.

2 Add the beef and cook for a further 2–3 minutes, until lightly colored. Stir in the lemongrass and ginger.

3 Remove the beef from the wok with a slotted spoon and set aside. Add the red and green bell peppers and onion to the wok and cook over a high heat for 2–3 minutes, until the onion is just turning golden brown and has softened slightly.

4 Return the beef to the pan, stir in the lime juice and season with salt and pepper to taste. Serve with noodles or rice.

NUTRITION
Calories 230; Sugars 4 g; Protein 26 g; Carbohydrate 6 g; Fat 12 g; Saturates 3 g

moderate

5 mins

10 mins

🍴 COOK'S TIP

When preparing lemongrass, take care to remove the outer layers, which can be tough. Use only the tender center part, which has the finest flavor.

The green of the beans complements the dark color of the beef, which is served in a rich sauce.

Beef *and* Beans

1 To make the marinade, mix together the cornstarch, soy sauce, and peanut oil in a small bowl.

2 Place the steak in a shallow glass bowl. Pour the marinade over the steak, turn to coat thoroughly, cover and marinate in the refrigerator for at least 30 minutes—the longer the better.

3 To make the sauce, heat the oil in a preheated wok or large, heavy-based skillet. Add the garlic, onion, beans, cashews, and bamboo shoots, and cook for 2–3 minutes.

4 Remove the steak from the marinade, using a slotted spoon. Reserve the marinade, then drain the steak, and add the meat to the wok, and cook for 3–4 minutes.

5 Mix together the soy sauce, Chinese rice wine, and beef bouillon. Blend the cornstarch with the water and add to the marinade, mixing well to combine.

6 Stir the mixture into the wok and bring the sauce to a boil, stirring, until it has thickened and cleared. Reduce the heat and let simmer for 2–3 minutes. Season with salt and pepper to taste and serve immediately.

SERVES 4

1 lb/450 g beef fillet steak or rump steak, cut into 1-inch/2.5-cm pieces

marinade
2 tsp cornstarch
2 tbsp dark soy sauce
2 tsp peanut oil

sauce
2 tbsp vegetable oil
3 garlic cloves, crushed
1 small onion, cut into 8 pieces
8 oz/225 g fine green beans, halved
1/4 cup unsalted cashews
1 oz/25 g canned bamboo shoots, drained
2 tsp dark soy sauce
2 tsp Chinese rice wine or dry sherry
1/2 cup beef bouillon
2 tsp cornstarch
4 tsp water
salt and pepper

NUTRITION
Calories *381*; Sugars *3 g*; Protein *25 g*;
Carbohydrate *10 g*; Fat *27 g*; Saturates *8 g*

easy

35 mins

15 mins

This recipe looks stunning if you arrange the ingredients on a serving platter, rather than toss them together.

Beef *and* Peanut Salad

SERVES 4

½ head Napa cabbage, shredded
1 large carrot, cut into matchsticks
4 oz/115 g radishes, quartered
3½ oz/100 g baby corn cobs, halved lengthwise
1 tbsp peanut oil
1 fresh red chile, seeded and chopped
1 garlic clove, chopped finely
12 oz/350 g lean beef, such as fillet, sirloin or rump, trimmed and finely shredded
1 tbsp dark soy sauce
¼ cup fresh peanuts, optional
sliced fresh red chile, to garnish

dressing
1 tbsp smooth peanut butter
1 tsp superfine sugar
2 tbsp light soy sauce
1 tbsp sherry vinegar
salt and pepper

NUTRITION
Calories *194*; Sugars *3 g*; Protein *21 g*;
Carbohydrate *5 g*; Fat *10 g*; Saturates *3 g*

⭐⭐ easy
🕐 10 mins
🕐 10 mins

1 Arrange the Napa cabbage, carrot, radishes, and baby corn cobs around the edge of a serving platter and set aside.

2 Heat the peanut oil in a preheated wok or large, heavy-based skillet until really hot.

3 Add the red chile, garlic, and beef to the wok and cook for 5 minutes.

4 Add the dark soy sauce and cook for another 1–2 minutes, until the meat is tender and cooked through.

5 Meanwhile, make the dressing. Place all of the ingredients in a small bowl and blend them together until smooth.

6 Place the hot cooked beef in the center of the salad ingredients. Spoon over the dressing and sprinkle with a few peanuts, if using. Garnish with the red chile and serve immediately.

COOK'S TIP

You can use chicken, turkey, lean pork, or even strips of venison instead of beef in this recipe.

A quick-and-easy stir-fry
for any day of the week,
this simple beef recipe is
a good one-pan entrée.

Beef *with* Beansprouts

1 Heat the oil in a preheated wok or large, heavy-based skillet over a high
heat. Add the scallions, reserving a few to garnish, garlic, and ginger, then
cook for 2–3 minutes, until softened. Add the beef and continue to cook for
4–5 minutes, until browned evenly.

2 Add the red bell pepper and cook for another 3–4 minutes. Add the chile and
beansprouts and cook for 2 minutes. Mix together the lemongrass, peanut
butter, coconut milk, rice wine vinegar, soy sauce, and sugar, then pour the
mixture into the wok and stir.

3 Meanwhile, cook the egg noodles in boiling, lightly salted water for
4 minutes, or according to the package directions. Drain the noodles and stir
into the wok, tossing to mix evenly.

4 Season with salt and pepper to taste. Sprinkle with the reserved scallions
and serve hot.

SERVES 4

2 tbsp sunflower oil
1 bunch scallions, sliced thinly
1 garlic clove, crushed
1 tsp chopped finely fresh gingerroot
1 lb 2 oz/500 g tender beef, cut into
    thin strips
1 large red bell pepper, seeded and sliced
1 small fresh red chile, seeded and chopped
3⅓ cups beansprouts
1 small lemongrass stem, chopped finely
2 tbsp smooth peanut butter
4 tbsp coconut milk
1 tbsp rice wine vinegar
1 tbsp soy sauce
1 tsp soft light brown sugar
9 oz/250 g dried medium egg noodles
salt and pepper

NUTRITION
Calories *140*; Sugars *3 g*; Protein *3 g*;
Fat *17 g*; Carbohydrate *20 g*; Saturates *1 g*

easy

15 mins

20 mins

Fish *and* Seafood

Throughout the Far Eastern countries, fish and seafood play a major role in the diet of the native people; this is because these foods are both plentiful and very healthy. They are also very versatile: there are many different ways of cooking fish and seafood in a wok—they may be steamed, deep-fried, or cooked with a range of delicious spices and sauces.

Japan is famed for its sushimi, or raw fish, but this is just one of the wide range of fish dishes served. Fish and seafood are offered at every meal in Japan, many of them cooked in a wok.

When buying fish and seafood for the recipes in this chapter, freshness is imperative to flavor, so be sure to buy and use the fish that you have chosen as soon as possible, preferably on the same day as buying it.

Fish and fruit is a classic Chinese combination, and this dish is no exception with its tropical fruity flavor.

Stir-Fried Cod *with* Mango

SERVES 4

2 tbsp vegetable oil
1 red onion, sliced
2 carrots, sliced into thin sticks
1 red bell pepper, seeded and sliced
1 green bell pepper, seeded and sliced
1 lb/450 g cod fillet, skinned and cubed
1 ripe mango, peeled, pitted and sliced
1 tsp cornstarch
1 tbsp light soy sauce
generous ⅓ cup tropical fruit juice
1 tbsp lime juice
1 tbsp chopped fresh cilantro, to garnish

1 Heat the oil in a preheated wok or large, heavy-based skillet and cook the onion, carrots, and red and green bell peppers for 5 minutes.

2 Add the cod and mango to the wok and cook for another 4–5 minutes, or until the fish is cooked through. (Be careful not to break the fish up.)

3 Mix together the cornstarch, soy sauce, fruit juice, and lime juice. Pour the mixture into the wok and stir until the mixture bubbles and the juices thicken. Scatter with cilantro and serve immediately on warm serving plates.

NUTRITION
Calories *200*; Sugars *12 g*; Protein *21 g*;
Carbohydrate *14 g*; Fat *7 g*; Saturates *1 g*

easy

10 mins

15 mins

 COOK'S TIP

You can use papaya as an alternative to the mango, if you prefer.

Szechuan pepper is quite hot and should be used sparingly to avoid making the dish too spicy.

Szechuan White Fish

1 Beat together the egg, flour, wine, and 1 tablespoon of the soy sauce to make a batter. Dip the cubes of fish into the batter to coat well.

2 Heat the oil in a preheated wok or large, heavy-based skillet. Reduce the heat slightly and cook the fish, in batches, for 2–3 minutes, until golden brown. Remove with a slotted spoon, drain on paper towels, set aside, and keep warm.

3 Pour all but 1 tablespoon of the oil from the wok and return it to the heat. Add the garlic, ginger, onion, celery, chile, and scallions, and cook for 1–2 minutes. Stir in the remaining soy sauce and the rice wine vinegar.

4 Add the Szechuan pepper, fish bouillon, and superfine sugar to the wok. Mix the cornstarch with the water to form a smooth paste and stir it into the bouillon. Bring to a boil and cook, stirring, for 1 minute, until the sauce has thickened and cleared.

5 Return the cooked fish to the wok and cook for another 1–2 minutes. Serve immediately.

SERVES 4

1 small egg, beaten
3 tbsp all-purpose flour
4 tbsp dry white wine
3 tbsp light soy sauce
12 oz/350 g white fish fillets, cut into
    1½-inch/4-cm cubes
vegetable oil, for frying
1 garlic clove, cut into slivers
1 tsp finely chopped fresh gingerroot
1 onion, chopped finely
1 celery stalk, chopped
1 fresh red chile, chopped
3 scallions, chopped
1 tsp rice wine vinegar
½ tsp ground Szechuan pepper
¾ cup fish bouillon
1 tsp superfine sugar
1 tsp cornstarch
2 tsp water

NUTRITION
Calories 140; Sugars 3 g; Protein 3 g;
Carbohydrate 20 g; Fat 17 g; Saturates 1 g

easy

15 mins

20 mins

Fish curries are sensational and this curry is no exception. Red curry and coconut are fantastic flavors with the fish.

Fish *with* Coconut *and* Basil

SERVES 4

2 tbsp vegetable oil
3 tbsp seasoned flour
1 lb/450 g cod fillet, skinned and cubed
1 clove garlic, crushed
2 tbsp red curry paste
1 tbsp fish sauce
1¼ cups coconut milk
6 oz/175 g cherry tomatoes, halved
20 fresh basil leaves, torn coarsely
fragrant rice, to serve

1 Heat the vegetable oil in a preheated wok or large, heavy-based skillet.

2 Place the seasoned flour in a bowl. Add the cubes of fish and mix well until thoroughly coated.

3 Add the fish to the wok and cook over a high heat for 3–4 minutes, or until the fish begins to brown at the edges.

4 In a small bowl, mix together the garlic, curry paste, fish sauce, and coconut milk. Pour the mixture over the fish and bring to a boil.

5 Reduce the heat, add the tomatoes to the mixture in the wok and let simmer for 5 minutes.

6 Add the basil to the wok and stir carefully to combine, taking care not to break up the cubes of fish or tomatoes.

7 Transfer the curry to serving plates and serve hot with fragrant rice.

NUTRITION
Calories *209*; Sugars *10 g*; Protein *21 g*;
Carbohydrate *15 g*; Fat *8 g*; Saturates *1 g*

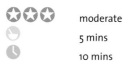

moderate

5 mins

10 mins

COOK'S TIP

Take care not to overcook the dish once the tomatoes are added, otherwise they will break down and the skins will come away.

This is a very hot dish—not for the fainthearted! It can be made without the chile flavorings, if preferred.

Crispy Fish

1 To make the batter, sift the all-purpose flour into a mixing bowl and make a well in the center. Add the egg yolk and peanut oil to the mixing bowl and gradually stir in the milk, incorporating the flour to form a smooth batter. Let stand for about 20 minutes.

2 Whisk the egg white until it forms soft peaks and fold it into the batter until thoroughly incorporated.

3 Heat the vegetable oil in a preheated wok or large, heavy-based skillet. Dip the fish into the batter and fry, in batches, for 8–10 minutes, until cooked through. Remove the fish from the wok with a slotted spoon, set aside, and keep warm until required.

4 Pour all but 1 tablespoon of the oil from the wok and return it to the heat. Add the chile, garlic, chili powder, tomato paste, rice wine vinegar, soy sauce, Chinese rice wine, water, and sugar, and cook, stirring, for 3–4 minutes.

5 Return the fish to the wok and stir gently to coat it in the sauce. Cook for 2–3 minutes, until hot. Transfer to a serving dish and serve immediately.

SERVES 4

vegetable oil, for deep-frying
1 lb/450 g white fish fillets, cut into
   1-inch/2.5-cm, cubes

batter
scant ½ cup all-purpose flour
1 egg, separated
1 tbsp peanut oil
4 tbsp milk

sauce
1 fresh red chile, chopped
2 garlic cloves, crushed
pinch of chili powder
3 tbsp tomato paste
1 tbsp rice wine vinegar
2 tbsp dark soy sauce
2 tbsp Chinese rice wine
2 tbsp water
pinch of superfine sugar

NUTRITION
Calories *281*; Sugars *3 g*; Protein *25 g*;
Carbohydrate *15 g*; Fat *12 g*; Saturates *2 g*

✪✪✪   moderate

⏱   30 mins

⏱   40 mins

This dish is a real treat and is perfect for special occasions. Monkfish has a tender flavor, which is ideal with asparagus, chili, and ginger.

Gingered Monkfish

SERVES 4

1 tbsp grated fresh gingerroot
2 tbsp sweet chili sauce
1 lb/450 g monkfish, cut into bite-size pieces
1 tbsp corn oil
3½ oz/100 g fine asparagus
3 scallions, sliced
1 tsp sesame oil

1 Mix together the ginger and the sweet chili sauce in a small bowl until they are thoroughly blended. Brush the ginger and chili sauce mixture over the monkfish pieces, using a pastry brush.

2 Heat the corn oil in a preheated wok or large, heavy-based skillet.

3 Add the monkfish, asparagus, and scallions to the wok and cook for about 5 minutes, stirring gently so the fish pieces and asparagus do not break up.

4 Remove the wok from the heat, drizzle the sesame oil over the stir-fry and toss well to combine.

5 Transfer the monkfish to warm serving plates and serve immediately.

NUTRITION

Calories *133*; Sugars *0 g*; Protein *21 g*;
Carbohydrate *1 g*; Fat *5 g*; Saturates *1 g*

easy

5 mins

10 mins

🍳 **COOK'S TIP**

Monkfish is quite expensive, but it is well worth using as it has a wonderful flavor and texture. You could use cubes of chunky cod fillet instead.

Salmon is marinated in a deliciously rich, sweet sauce, stir-fried, and served on a bed of crispy leeks.

Stir-Fried Salmon *with* Leeks

1 Place the slices of salmon in a shallow, non-metallic dish.

2 Mix together the soy sauce, tomato catsup, rice wine vinegar, sugar, and garlic in a small bowl.

3 Pour the mixture over the salmon, toss well and marinate in the refrigerator for about 30 minutes.

4 Meanwhile, heat 3 tablespoons of the corn oil in a preheated wok, or large, heavy-based skillet.

5 Add the leeks to the wok and cook over a medium–high heat for about 10 minutes, or until the leeks become crispy and tender.

6 Using a slotted spoon, carefully remove the leeks from the wok and transfer to warmed serving plates.

7 Add the remaining oil to the wok. Add the salmon and the marinade to the wok and cook for 2 minutes.

8 Remove the salmon from the wok and arrange on top of the leeks, garnish with the red chiles, and serve immediately.

SERVES 4

1 lb/450 g salmon fillet, skinned and sliced
2 tbsp sweet soy sauce
2 tbsp tomato catsup
1 tsp rice wine vinegar
1 tbsp raw brown sugar
1 garlic clove, crushed
4 tbsp corn oil
1 lb/450 g leeks, shredded thinly
finely chopped red chiles, to garnish

NUTRITION
Calories *360*; Sugars *9 g*; Protein *24 g*;
Carbohydrate *11 g*; Fat *25 g*; Saturates *4 g*

⭐⭐   easy

🕐   40 mins

🕐   15 mins

Five-spice is a blend of star anise, fennel, cinnamon, cloves, and Szechuan peppercorns. It is a popular addition to Chinese cooking.

Five-Spice Salmon

SERVES 4

2 tsp ground Chinese five-spice
4 salmon fillets, skinned, about
    4½ oz/125 g each
1 large leek, shredded
1 large carrot, cut into thin strips
4 oz/115 g snow peas, shredded
1-inch/2.5-cm piece fresh gingerroot,
    shredded
2 tbsp ginger wine
2 tbsp light soy sauce
1 tbsp vegetable oil
salt and pepper

to garnish
shredded leek
shredded fresh gingerroot
shredded carrot

1 Rub the Chinese five-spice into both sides of the fish and season with salt and pepper. Set aside until required.

2 Place the vegetables in a large bowl and add the ginger, ginger wine and 1 tablespoon of the soy sauce.

3 Preheat the broiler to medium. Place the salmon fillets on the rack and brush with the remaining soy sauce. Cook for 2–3 minutes on each side, until cooked through.

4 While the salmon is cooking, heat the oil in a preheated wok or large, heavy-based skillet and cook the vegetables for 5 minutes, until just tender. (Take care that you do not overcook the vegetables—they should still have bite.) Transfer the vegetables to serving plates and place the salmon on top. Garnish with shredded leek, ginger, and carrot and serve.

NUTRITION
Calories 267; Sugars 3 g; Protein 24 g;
Carbohydrate 4 g; Fat 17 g; Saturates 3 g

easy

15 mins

6 mins

🍳 **COOK'S TIP**

Chinese five-spice has a strong, pungent flavor and should be used in moderation.

The fish in this fragrant, curry-like stew can be varied according to taste or availability, but do stick to fish that stays firm when cooked.

Spicy Thai Seafood Stew

1 Heat the oil in a preheated wok or large, heavy-based skillet and cook the shallots, garlic, and curry paste for 1–2 minutes. Add the lemongrass and shrimp paste, stir in the coconut milk, and bring to a boil.

2 Reduce the heat, then add the squid, white fish, and shrimp to the wok, and simmer for 2 minutes.

3 Add the clams and simmer for another minute until the clams open. Discard any clams that do not open.

4 Scatter the shredded basil leaves over the stew, and serve immediately, garnished with whole basil leaves and with fragrant rice.

SERVES 4

1 tbsp sunflower oil
4 shallots, chopped finely
2 garlic cloves, chopped finely
2 tbsp Thai green curry paste
2 small lemongrass stems, chopped finely
1 tsp shrimp paste
scant 2 1/4 cups coconut milk
7 oz/200 g squid, cut into rings
1 lb 2 oz/500 g firm white fish fillet, preferably monkfish or halibut, cubed
7 oz/200 g peeled, raw jumbo shrimp, de-veined
12 fresh clams in shells, cleaned
8 basil leaves, shredded finely, plus extra whole leaves, to garnish
boiled fragrant rice, to serve

NUTRITION
Calories 267; Sugars 7 g; Protein 42 g; Carbohydrate 9 g; Fat 7 g; Saturates 1 g

⭐⭐⭐   moderate

🕐   10 mins

🕐   10 mins

👨‍🍳 **COOK'S TIP**

If you prefer, fresh mussels in shells can be used instead of clams—add them in step 3 and follow the recipe as directed.

Fresh tuna is a dark, meaty fish, and is now widely available. It lends itself perfectly to the rich flavors in this recipe.

Tuna *and* Vegetable Stir-Fry

SERVES 4

2 tbsp corn oil
3 small carrots, cut into thin sticks
1 onion, sliced
6 oz/175 g baby corn cobs, halved lengthwise
6 oz/175 g snow peas
1 lb/450 g fresh tuna, sliced thinly
2 tbsp fish sauce
1 tbsp palm sugar
finely grated zest and juice of 1 orange
2 tbsp sherry
1 tsp cornstarch
boiled rice or noodles, to serve

1 Heat the corn oil in a preheated wok or large, heavy-based skillet.

2 Add the carrots, onion, baby corn cobs, and snow peas to the wok and cook for 5 minutes.

3 Add the tuna to the wok and cook for about 2–3 minutes, or until the tuna turns opaque.

4 Mix together the fish sauce, palm sugar, orange zest and juice, sherry, and cornstarch until well blended.

5 Pour the mixture over the tuna and vegetables and cook for 2 minutes, or until the juices thicken. Serve the stir-fry with rice or noodles.

NUTRITION
Calories 245; Sugars 11 g; Protein 30 g;
Carbohydrate 14 g; Fat 7 g; Saturates 1 g

easy

10 mins

10 mins

COOK'S TIP

Try using swordfish steaks instead of the tuna. Swordfish steaks are now widely available and are similar in texture to tuna.

Fan-tail shrimp make any meal a special occasion, especially when cooked in such a delicious crispy coating.

Coconut Shrimp

1 Mix together the shredded coconut, white breadcrumbs, Chinese five-spice, salt, and lime zest in a bowl.

2 Lightly whisk the egg white in a separate bowl.

3 Rinse the shrimp under cold running water, and pat dry with paper towels.

4 Dip the shrimp into the egg white, then into the coconut and bread crumb mixture, so that they are evenly coated.

5 Heat about 2 inches/5 cm of sunflower or corn oil in a preheated wok or large, heavy-based pan.

6 Add the shrimp to the wok and cook for about 5 minutes, or until golden and crispy. Remove the shrimp with a slotted spoon and let drain on paper towels.

7 Transfer the coconut shrimp to warm serving dishes and garnish with lemon wedges. Serve immediately with soy or chili sauce.

SERVES 4

½ cup shredded coconut
½ cup fresh white bread crumbs
1 tsp ground Chinese five-spice
½ tsp salt
finely grated zest of 1 lime
1 egg white
1 lb/450 g raw fan-tail shrimp
sunflower or corn oil, for frying
lemon wedges, to garnish
soy or chili sauce, to serve

NUTRITION
Calories *236*; Sugars *1 g*; Protein *27 g*; Carbohydrate *3 g*; Fat *13 g*; Saturates *7 g*

easy
5 mins
10 mins

COOK'S TIP

Chinese five-spice will keep for a few months if stored in a dark, cool place, in an airtight container.

Hot and spicy, these shrimp, coated in a crunchy batter, make a delicious appetizer or party food.

Szechuan Shrimp

SERVES 4

pinch of salt
½ egg white, beaten lightly
1 tsp cornstarch
9–10½ oz/250–300 g peeled, raw jumbo shrimp
2½ cups vegetable oil
fresh cilantro leaves, to garnish

Sauce
1 tsp chopped finely fresh gingerroot
2 scallions, chopped finely
1 garlic clove, chopped finely
3–4 small dried red chilis, seeded and chopped
1 tbsp light soy sauce
1 tsp Chinese rice wine or dry sherry
1 tbsp tomato paste
1 tbsp oyster sauce
2–3 tbsp vegetable bouillon or water
a few drops of sesame oil

1 Mix together the salt, egg white, and cornstarch to make a paste, then add the shrimp and turn until well coated in the mixture.

2 Heat the oil in a preheated wok or large, heavy-based skillet until it is smoking, then deep-fry the shrimp for about 1 minute. Remove with a slotted spoon and drain on paper towels.

3 Pour all but 1 tablespoon of the oil from the wok. Add all the ingredients for the sauce, bring to a boil, and stir until smooth and well blended.

4 Add the shrimp to the sauce and stir until well coated.

5 Serve the shrimp, garnished with fresh cilantro leaves.

NUTRITION
Calories *140*; Sugars *3 g*; Protein *3 g*;
Carbohydrate *20 g*; Fat *17 g*; Saturates *1 g*

easy

15 mins

15 mins

🌀 **COOK'S TIP**

Raw shrimp should be used if possible, otherwise add ready-cooked shrimp at the beginning of step 3.

Basil and tomatoes are ideal flavorings for shrimp, which are also spiced with cumin seeds and garlic in this dish.

Shrimp *with* Spicy Tomatoes

1 Heat the corn oil in a preheated wok or large, heavy-based skillet.

2 Add the onion and garlic to the wok and cook over a medium heat for 2–3 minutes, or until softened.

3 Stir in the cumin seeds and cook for 1 minute.

4 Add the sugar, chopped tomatoes, and sun-dried tomato paste to the wok. Bring the mixture to a boil, then reduce the heat and let the sauce simmer for 10 minutes.

5 Add the basil, shrimp, and season with salt and pepper to taste. Increase the heat and cook for a further 2–3 minutes, or until the shrimp are completely cooked through.

SERVES 4

2 tbsp corn oil
1 onion, chopped finely
2 garlic cloves, crushed
1 tsp cumin seeds
1 tbsp brown sugar
14 oz/400 g canned chopped tomatoes
1 tbsp sun-dried tomato paste
1 tbsp chopped fresh basil
1 lb/450 g peeled, cooked jumbo shrimp
salt and pepper

NUTRITION
Calories 237; Sugar 9 g; Protein 27 g; Carbohydrate 11 g; Fat 10 g; Saturates 1 g

⭐⭐　　easy
🕐　　2 mins
🕐　　20 mins

COOK'S TIP

Always heat your wok before you add oil or other ingredients. This will prevent anything from sticking to it.

Crispy ginger is a
wonderful garnish and
offsets the spicy shrimp
both visually and in flavor.

Shrimp *with* Ginger

SERVES 4

oil, for frying
2-inch/5-cm piece fresh
  gingerroot, shredded
1 onion, diced
3 small carrots, diced
1 cup frozen peas
1 cup beansprouts
1 tsp ground Chinese five-spice
1 tbsp tomato paste
1 tbsp soy sauce
1 lb/450 g peeled, raw jumbo shrimp

1 Heat about 1 inch/2.5 cm of oil in a preheated wok or large, heavy-based skillet. Add the ginger and cook for 1 minute, or until the ginger is crisp. Remove the ginger with a slotted spoon and let drain on paper towels.

2 Drain all but 2 tablespoons of the oil from the wok. Add the onion and carrots to the wok and cook for 5 minutes. Add the peas and beansprouts and cook for another 2 minutes.

3 Combine the Chinese five-spice, tomato paste, and soy sauce. Brush the mixture over the shrimp.

4 Add the shrimp to the wok and cook for a further 2 minutes, or until the shrimp are completely cooked through. Transfer the shrimp mixture to a warm serving bowl and top with the crispy ginger. Serve immediately.

NUTRITION

Calories 140; Sugars 3 g; Protein 3 g;
Carbohydrate 20 g; Fat 17 g; Saturates 1 g

easy

15 mins

15 mins

🖫 **COOK'S TIP**

Use slices of firm, white fish instead of the jumbo shrimp, if you wish.

The classic ingredients of this popular dish are eggs, carrots, and small shrimp. Add extra ingredients, such as peas or crabmeat, if desired.

Shrimp Foo Yung

1 Heat the vegetable oil in a preheated wok or large, heavy-based skillet, swirling it around until really hot.

2 Add the carrot and cook for 1–2 minutes, until just tender.

3 Push the carrot to one side of the wok and add the beaten eggs. Cook, stirring gently, for 1–2 minutes.

4 Stir the small shrimp, light soy sauce, and Chinese five-spice powder into the mixture in the wok. Stir-fry the mixture for 2–3 minutes, or until the small shrimp change color and the mixture is almost dry in consistency.

5 Turn the small shrimp out on to warm plates and sprinkle the scallions, sesame seeds, and sesame oil on top. Serve immediately.

SERVES 4

2 tbsp vegetable oil
1 carrot, grated
5 eggs, beaten
8 oz/225 g peeled, raw small shrimp
1 tbsp light soy sauce
pinch of ground Chinese five-spice
2 scallions, chopped
2 tsp sesame seeds
1 tsp sesame oil

NUTRITION
Calories *240*; Sugars *1 g*; Protein *22 g*; Carbohydrate *1 g*; Fat *16 g*; Saturates *3 g*

easy

5 mins

10 mins

COOK'S TIP

Mix water with the egg in step 3 for a lighter omelet.

This shrimp dish is very
quick and simple, and is
ideal for supper or lunch
when time is short.

Cantonese Shrimp

SERVES 4

5 tbsp vegetable oil
4 garlic cloves, crushed
1½ lb/675 g peeled, raw shrimp, de-veined
4 tsp chopped fresh gingerroot
6 oz/175 g lean pork, diced
1 leek, sliced
2 tbsp Chinese rice wine or dry sherry
2 tbsp light soy sauce
2 tsp superfine sugar
²⁄₃ cup fish bouillon
4½ tsp cornstarch
3 tbsp water
3 eggs, beaten

to garnish
shredded leek
sliced red bell pepper

NUTRITION
Calories *460*; Sugar *3 g*; Protein *53 g*;
Carbohydrate *6 g*; Fat *24 g*; Saturates *5 g*

moderate

10 mins

20 mins

1 Heat 2 tablespoons of the vegetable oil in a preheated wok or large, heavy-based skillet.

2 Add the garlic to the wok and cook for 30 seconds.

3 Add the shrimp and cook for 5 minutes, or until they change color. Remove the shrimp from the wok with a slotted spoon, set aside and keep warm.

4 Add the remaining oil to the wok and heat, carefully swirling it around the bottom of the wok until really hot.

5 Add the ginger, pork, and leek to the wok and cook over a medium heat for 4–5 minutes, or until the pork is lightly colored and seared.

6 Add the rice wine, soy sauce, superfine sugar, and fish bouillon to the wok and stir to blend.

7 In a small bowl, blend the cornstarch with the water to form a smooth paste and stir it into the wok. Cook, stirring, until the sauce thickens and clears.

8 Return the shrimp to the wok and add the beaten eggs. Cook for 5–6 minutes, gently stirring occasionally, until the eggs set.

9 Transfer to a warm serving dish, garnished with the leek and bell pepper.

Scallops have a terrific, subtle flavor, which is complemented in this dish by the buttery sauce.

Seared Scallops

1 Heat the vegetable oil in a preheated wok or large, heavy-based skillet, swirling the oil around the bottom of the wok until it is really hot.

2 Add the green chile, scallions, and scallops to the wok, and cook over a high heat for 4–5 minutes, or until the scallops are just cooked through. If using frozen scallops, be sure not to overcook them as they will begin to disintegrate.

3 Add the soy sauce and butter to the scallop stir-fry and heat through until the butter melts.

4 Transfer to warm serving bowls and serve hot.

SERVES 4

2 tbsp vegetable oil
1 fresh green chile, seeded and sliced
6 scallions, sliced
1 lb/450 g fresh scallops, without roe, or the same quantity frozen scallops, thawed thoroughly and halved horizontally
3 tbsp sweet soy sauce
2 tbsp butter, cubed

NUTRITION
Calories 272; Sugars 0 g; Protein 28 g;
Carbohydrate 2 g; Fat 17 g; Saturates 8 g

⭐ very easy
🕐 10 mins
🕐 10 mins

👨‍🍳 COOK'S TIP

You could use shrimp or shelled clams instead of the scallops, if you prefer.

Scallops are both attractive and delicious. Cooked with ginger and orange, this dish is perfect served with plain boiled rice.

Scallops *in* Ginger Sauce

SERVES 4

2 tbsp vegetable oil

1 lb/450 g fresh scallops, or the same quantity frozen, defrosted thoroughly, halved

2 tsp finely chopped fresh gingerroot

3 garlic cloves, crushed

2 leeks, shredded

¾ cup frozen peas

4½ oz/125 g canned bamboo shoots, drained and rinsed

2 tbsp light soy sauce

2 tbsp unsweetened orange juice

1 tsp superfine sugar

orange zest, to garnish

1 Heat the vegetable oil in a preheated wok or large, heavy-based skillet. Add the scallops and cook for 1–2 minutes. Remove the scallops from the wok with a slotted spoon, keep warm and set aside until required.

2 Add the ginger and garlic to the wok and cook for 30 seconds. Stir in the leeks and peas and cook, stirring, for another 2 minutes.

3 Add the bamboo shoots and return the scallops to the wok. Stir gently to mix without breaking up the scallops.

4 Stir in the soy sauce, orange juice, and superfine sugar and cook for 1–2 minutes.

5 Transfer the scallop stir-fry to a serving dish, garnish with the orange zest and serve immediately.

NUTRITION

Calories *216*; Sugars *4 g*; Protein *30 g*; Carbohydrate *8 g*; Fat *8 g*; Saturates *1 g*

easy

5 mins

10 mins

🍳 COOK'S TIP

The edible parts of a scallop are the round white muscle and the orange and white coral or roe. The frilly skirt surrounding the muscle—the gills and mantle—can be used for a shellfish bouillon; other parts should be discarded.

This dish looks so impressive, the combination of colors making it look almost too good to eat!

Mussels *in* Black Bean Sauce

1 Place the green-lipped mussels in a large bowl, sprinkle with the cumin seeds and toss well to coat. Set aside until required.

2 Heat the vegetable oil in a preheated wok or large, heavy-based skillet, swirling the oil around the bottom of the wok until it is really hot.

3 Add the leeks, garlic, and red bell pepper to the wok and cook for 5 minutes, or until the vegetables are tender.

4 Add the bamboo shoots, baby spinach leaves, and cooked green-lipped mussels to the wok and cook for about 2 minutes.

5 Pour the black bean sauce over the ingredients in the wok, toss well to coat in the sauce and let simmer for a few seconds, stirring occasionally.

6 Transfer the stir-fry to warm serving bowls and serve immediately.

SERVES 4

12 oz/350 g cooked, shelled
   green-lipped mussels
1 tsp cumin seeds
2 tbsp vegetable oil
12 oz/350 g leeks, shredded
2 garlic cloves, crushed
1 red bell pepper, seeded and sliced
1¾ oz/50 g canned bamboo shoots, drained
6 oz/175 g baby spinach leaves
5¾ oz/160 g jar black bean sauce

NUTRITION
Calories *174*; Sugars *4 g*; Protein *19 g*;
Carbohydrate *6 g*; Fat *8 g*; Saturates *1 g*

easy

5 mins

10 mins

COOK'S TIP

If fresh green-lipped mussels are not available, they can be bought shelled in cans and jars from most large food stores.

Oysters are more commonly eaten raw, but are just as delicious when quickly cooked and combined with citrus flavors, as in this recipe.

Oysters *with* Bean Curd

SERVES 4

2 tbsp sunflower oil
8 oz/225 g leeks, sliced
12 oz/350 g firm bean curd, cut into bite-size pieces
12 oz/350 g shelled oysters
2 tbsp fresh lemon juice
1 tsp cornstarch
2 tbsp light soy sauce
generous $\frac{1}{3}$ cup fish bouillon
2 tbsp chopped fresh cilantro
1 tsp finely grated lemon zest

1 Heat the sunflower oil in a preheated wok or large, heavy-based skillet. Add the leeks to the wok and cook for about 2 minutes.

2 Add the bean curd and oysters to the wok and cook for 1–2 minutes.

3 Mix together the lemon juice, cornstarch, light soy sauce, and fish bouillon in a small bowl, stirring until well blended.

4 Pour the cornstarch mixture into the wok and cook, stirring occasionally, until the juices start to thicken.

5 Transfer to serving bowls and scatter the cilantro and lemon zest on top. Serve immediately.

NUTRITION
Calories 175; Sugars 2 g; Protein 18 g; Carbohydrate 3 g; Fat 10 g; Saturates 1 g

easy

5 mins

10 mins

🍳 **COOK'S TIP**

Shelled clams or mussels could be used instead of the oysters, if you prefer.

The delicate flavor of Napa cabbage and crabmeat are enhanced by the coconut milk in this recipe.

Crab *with* Napa Cabbage

1 Heat the vegetable oil in a preheated wok or large, heavy-based skillet.

2 Add the mushrooms and garlic to the wok and cook for 3 minutes, or until the mushrooms have softened.

3 Add the scallions and Napa cabbage to the wok and cook until the leaves have wilted.

4 Mix together the mild curry paste and coconut milk in a small bowl.

5 Add the mixture to the wok, together with the crabmeat and chili flakes. Mix together until well combined. Heat the mixture in the wok until the juices start to bubble.

6 Transfer the crab and vegetable stir-fry to warm serving bowls.

SERVES 4

2 tbsp vegetable oil
8 oz/225 g shiitake mushrooms, sliced
2 garlic cloves, crushed
6 scallions, sliced
1 head Napa cabbage, shredded
1 tbsp mild curry paste
6 tbsp coconut milk
7 oz/200 g canned white crabmeat, drained
1 tsp dried chili flakes

NUTRITION
Calories *109*; Sugars *1 g*; Protein *11 g*;
Carbohydrate *2 g*; Fat *6 g*; Saturates *1 g*

easy

5 mins

10 mins

 COOK'S TIP

Shiitake mushrooms are now readily available in the fresh vegetable section of most large food stores.

Squid is really wonderful if quickly cooked as in this recipe, and contrary to popular belief it is not tough and rubbery unless it is overcooked.

Squid *with* Black Bean Sauce

SERVES 4

1 lb/450 g squid rings
2 tbsp all-purpose flour
½ tsp salt
2 tbsp peanut oil
1 green bell pepper, sliced
1 red onion, sliced
5¾ oz/160 g jar black bean sauce

1 Rinse the squid rings under cold running water and pat dry thoroughly with paper towels.

2 Place the all-purpose flour and salt in a bowl and mix together. Add the squid rings and toss until they are evenly coated.

3 Heat the peanut oil in a preheated wok or large, heavy-based skillet, swirling the oil around the bottom of the wok until it is really hot.

4 Add the green bell pepper and red onion to the wok and cook for about 2 minutes, or until the vegetables have softened.

5 Add the squid rings to the wok and cook for another 5 minutes, or until the squid is cooked through. (Be careful not to overcook the squid.)

6 Add the black bean sauce to the wok and heat through until the juices are bubbling. Transfer the squid stir-fry to warm serving bowls.

NUTRITION

Calories *180*; Sugars *2 g*; Protein *19 g*;
Carbohydrate *10 g*; Fat *7 g*; Saturates *1 g*

easy

5 mins

8 mins

🍲 COOK'S TIP

Serve this recipe with fried rice or noodles, tossed in soy sauce, if you wish.

Squid is a delicious seafood, which, if prepared and cooked correctly, is a quick-cooking, attractive, and tasty ingredient.

Squid *with* Oyster Sauce

1 To prepare the squid, cut down the center of the body lengthwise. Flatten the squid out, inside uppermost, and score a lattice design deep into the flesh, using a sharp knife.

2 To make the sauce, combine the oyster sauce, soy sauce, sugar, and garlic in a small bowl. Stir to dissolve the sugar and set aside until required.

3 Heat the oil in a preheated wok or large, heavy-based skillet until almost smoking. Reduce the heat slightly, add the squid and cook until they curl up. Remove with a slotted spoon and drain thoroughly on paper towels.

4 Pour all but 2 tablespoons of the oil from the wok. Add the ginger and snow peas and cook for 1 minute.

5 Return the squid to the wok and pour in the sauce and hot fish bouillon. Let simmer for 3 minutes, until thickened. Transfer to a warm serving dish, garnish with red bell pepper triangles and serve immediately.

SERVES 4

1 lb/450 g squid
²⁄₃ cup vegetable oil
1 tsp grated fresh gingerroot
2 oz/55 g snow peas
5 tbsp hot fish bouillon
red bell pepper triangles, to garnish

sauce
1 tbsp oyster sauce
1 tbsp light soy sauce
pinch of superfine sugar
1 garlic clove, crushed

NUTRITION
Calories *320*; Sugars *1 g*; Protein *18 g*;
Carbohydrate *2 g*; Fat *26 g*; Saturates *3 g*

⭐⭐⭐   moderate
🕐   5 mins
🕐   10 mins

👹 **COOK'S TIP**

Take care not to overcook the squid, otherwise it will become rubbery and unappetizing.

Vegetables

Vegetables play an important role in wok and stir-fry cooking in the Far East and are used extensively in all meals. It is perfectly possible to enjoy a meal from a selection of the following recipes contained in this chapter without including meat or fish. Baby corn cobs, Napa cabbage and green beans, young spinach leaves, and bok choy can all bring a unique flavor and freshness to a stir-fried dish.

Native Far Eastern people enjoy their vegetables crisp, so cooking times in this chapter reflect this factor in order to bring out the flavors and textures of the ingredients used.

When selecting vegetables for cooking, great importance is attached to the freshness of the ingredients used. Always buy firm, crisp vegetables, and cook them as soon as possible after buying them. Another point to remember is to wash the vegetables just before cutting and to cook them as soon as they have been cut so that the vitamin content is not lost.

Napa cabbage is rather similar to lettuce in that the leaves are delicate with a sweet flavor.

Napa Cabbage *in* Honey

SERVES 4

1 tbsp peanut oil
1 tsp grated fresh gingerroot
2 garlic cloves, crushed
1 fresh red chile, sliced
1 lb/450 g Napa cabbage, shredded
1 tbsp Chinese rice wine or dry sherry
4½ tsp light soy sauce
1 tbsp clear honey
½ cup orange juice
1 tbsp sesame oil
2 tsp sesame seeds
orange zest, to garnish

1 Heat the peanut oil in a preheated wok or large, heavy-based skillet. Add the ginger, garlic, and chile to the wok and cook for about 30 seconds.

2 Add the Napa cabbage, Chinese rice wine, soy sauce, honey, and orange juice to the wok and bring to the boil. Reduce the heat and let simmer for 5 minutes.

3 Add the sesame oil and sesame seeds to the wok and mix well.

4 Transfer the stir-fry to a warm serving dish, garnish with the orange zest and serve immediately.

NUTRITION
Calories *121*; Sugars *6 g*; Protein *5 g*;
Carbohydrate *10 g*; Fat *7 g*; Saturates *1 g*

  easy

5 mins

10 mins

🍳 **COOK'S TIP**

Single-flower honey has a more individual flavor than blended honey. Acacia honey is typically Chinese, but you could also try clover, lemon blossom, lime flower, or orange blossom honey.

Warm cucumbers are absolutely delicious, especially when combined with the heat of chile and the flavor of ginger.

Stir-Fried Chile Cucumber

1 Peel the cucumbers and cut in half lengthwise. Scrape the seeds from the center with a teaspoon or melon baller and discard.

2 Cut the cucumber into strips and place on a plate. Sprinkle the salt over the cucumber strips and set aside for 20 minutes. Rinse well under cold running water and pat dry with paper towels.

3 Heat the vegetable oil in a preheated wok or large, heavy-based skillet until it is almost smoking. Reduce the heat slightly and add the garlic, ginger, chiles, and scallions, and cook for 30 seconds.

4 Add the cucumber to the wok, together with the yellow bean sauce and honey and cook for 30 seconds.

5 Add the water and cook over a high heat until most of the water has evaporated.

6 Sprinkle the sesame oil over the stir-fry. Transfer to a warm serving dish and serve immediately.

SERVES 4

2 cucumbers
2 tsp salt
1 tbsp vegetable oil
2 garlic cloves, crushed
1 tsp grated fresh gingerroot
2 fresh red chiles, chopped
2 scallions, chopped
1 tsp yellow bean sauce
1 tbsp clear honey
½ cup water
1 tsp sesame oil

NUTRITION
Calories 67; Sugars 4 g; Protein 1 g;
Carbohydrate 5 g; Fat 5 g; Saturates 1 g

easy
30 mins
5 mins

👨‍🍳 **COOK'S TIP**

The cucumber is sprinkled with salt and left to stand in order to draw out the excess water, thus preventing a soggy meal!

These beans are cooked simply in a spicy, hot sauce for a tasty and very easy side dish.

Green Bean Stir-Fry

SERVES 4

2 tbsp peanut oil
1 lb/450 g fine green beans, halved
2 fresh red chiles, seeded and sliced
½ tsp ground star anise
1 garlic clove, crushed
2 tbsp light soy sauce
2 tsp clear honey
½ tsp sesame oil

1 Heat the oil in a preheated wok or large, heavy-based skillet until it is almost smoking.

2 Reduce the heat slightly, add the green beans and cook for 1 minute.

3 Add the red chiles, star anise, and garlic to the wok and cook for another 30 seconds.

4 Mix together the soy sauce, honey, and sesame oil in a small bowl.

5 Stir the sauce mixture into the wok. Cook for 2 minutes, tossing the beans to ensure that they are thoroughly coated in the sauce.

6 Transfer the mixture to a warm serving dish and serve immediately.

NUTRITION
Calories *86*; Sugars *4 g*; Protein *2 g*;
Carbohydrate *6 g*; Fat *6 g*; Saturates *1 g*

easy

5 mins

5 mins

🍲 COOK'S TIP

This recipe is surprisingly delicious made with Brussels sprouts instead of green beans. Trim the sprouts, then shred them finely. Cook the sprouts in hot oil for 2 minutes, then proceed with the recipe from step 2.

Ginger and broccoli make the perfect combination of flavors and colors. They also make an exceptionally tasty side dish.

Gingered Broccoli

1 Heat the peanut oil in a preheated wok or large, heavy-base skillet. Add the garlic and ginger and cook for 30 seconds.

2 Add the broccoli, leek, and water chestnuts and cook for another 3–4 minutes.

3 Add the superfine sugar, vegetable bouillon, and dark soy sauce to the wok and bring to the boil. Reduce the heat and let simmer for 4–5 minutes, or until the broccoli is almost cooked.

4 Blend the cornstarch with the water to form a smooth paste and stir it into the wok. Bring to a boil and cook, stirring constantly, for 1 minute, or until the sauce is thickened.

5 Transfer the vegetables to a serving dish and serve immediately.

SERVES 4

2 tbsp peanut oil
1 garlic clove, crushed
2-inch/5-cm piece fresh gingerroot, chopped or shredded finely
$1\frac{1}{2}$ lb/675 g broccoli florets
1 leek, sliced
$2\frac{3}{4}$ oz/75 g canned water chestnuts, drained and halved
$\frac{1}{2}$ tsp superfine sugar
$\frac{1}{2}$ cup vegetable bouillon
1 tsp dark soy sauce
1 tsp cornstarch
2 tsp water

NUTRITION

Calories *118*; Sugars *3 g*; Protein *8 g*; Carbohydrate *6 g*; Fat *7 g*; Saturates *1 g*

⭐⭐ easy
🕐 5 mins
🕐 15 mins

🧑‍🍳 **COOK'S TIP**

Use spinach instead of the broccoli: cut the stalks into 2-inch/5-cm lengths, keeping the leaves separate. Add the stalks with the leek in step 2 and add the leaves 2 minutes later. Reduce the cooking time in step 3 to 3–4 minutes.

The green lentils used in this recipe require soaking but it is worth the time for the flavor. If time is short, use red lentils, which do not require soaking.

Green Lentil Pan-Fry

SERVES 4

3¾ cups dried green lentils
4 tbsp butter or vegetarian margarine
2 garlic cloves, crushed
2 tbsp olive oil
1 tbsp cider vinegar
1 red onion, cut into 8 pieces
1¾ oz/50 g baby corn cobs,
  halved lengthwise
1 yellow bell pepper, seeded and
  cut into strips
1 red bell pepper, seeded and cut
  into strips
1¾ oz/50 g green beans, halved
½ cup vegetable bouillon
2 tbsp honey
salt and pepper
crusty bread, to serve

1 Soak the lentils in a large pan of cold water for 25 minutes. Bring to the boil, reduce the heat and simmer for 20 minutes. Drain thoroughly.

2 Add 1 tablespoon of the butter, 1 garlic clove, 1 tablespoon of oil, and the cider vinegar to the lentils and mix well.

3 Melt the remaining butter, garlic, and oil in a preheated wok or large, heavy-based skillet and cook the onion, baby corn cobs, yellow and red bell peppers, and beans for 3–4 minutes.

4 Add the vegetable bouillon and bring to a boil. Cook the mixture for about 10 minutes, or until the liquid has evaporated.

5 Add the honey and season with salt and pepper to taste. Stir in the lentil mixture and cook for 1 minute to heat through. Spoon on to warmed serving plates and serve with crusty bread.

NUTRITION
Calories 490; Sugars 12 g; Protein 26 g;
Carbohydrates 61 g; Fat 18 g; Saturates 8 g

⭐⭐ easy

🕐 30 mins

🕐 45 mins

🍳 **COOK'S TIP**

This stir-fry is very versatile—you can use a mixture of your favorite vegetables, if you prefer, such as zucchini, carrots, or snow peas.

In this recipe, spinach is fried with spices and then braised in a soy-flavored sauce with bamboo shoots for a rich, delicious dish.

Bamboo *with* Spinach

1 Heat the peanut oil in a preheated wok or large, heavy-based skillet, swirling the oil around the bottom of the wok until it is really hot.

2 Add the spinach and bamboo shoots to the wok and cook for 1 minute.

3 Add the garlic, chiles, and cinnamon to the mixture in the wok and cook for another 30 seconds.

4 Stir in the bouillon, sugar, salt, and light soy sauce, cover, and cook over a medium heat for 5 minutes, or until the vegetables are cooked through and the sauce has reduced. If there is too much cooking liquid, blend a little cornstarch with double the quantity of cold water and stir it into the sauce.

5 Transfer the bamboo shoots and spinach to a serving dish and serve.

SERVES 4

3 tbsp peanut oil
8 oz/225 g spinach, chopped
6 oz/175 g canned bamboo shoots, drained and rinsed
1 garlic clove, crushed
2 fresh red chiles, sliced
pinch of ground cinnamon
1 1/4 cups vegetable bouillon
pinch of sugar
pinch of salt
1 tbsp light soy sauce

NUTRITION
Calories *105*; Sugars *1 g*; Protein *3 g*; Carbohydrate *3 g*; Fat *9 g*; Saturates *2 g*

easy

5 mins

10 mins

COOK'S TIP

Fresh bamboo shoots are rarely available in the West. Canned bamboo shoots are quite satisfactory, as they are used to provide a crunchy texture, rather than for their flavor, which is fairly bland.

Dim sum are small Chinese parcels which may be filled with a variety of fillings, steamed or deep-fried, and served with a soy or plum dipping sauce.

Vegetable Dim Sum

SERVES 4

2 scallions, chopped
1 oz/25 g fine green beans, chopped
½ small carrot, chopped finely
¼ cup beansprouts, chopped
1 oz/25 g white mushrooms, chopped
1 fresh red chile, chopped
¼ cup unsalted cashews, chopped
1 small egg, beaten
2 tbsp cornstarch
1 tsp light soy sauce
1 tsp Peking sauce
1 tsp sesame oil
32 wonton wrappers
oil, for deep-frying
1 tbsp sesame seeds
soy sauce or plum sauce, for dipping

1 Mix all of the vegetables and chile together in a bowl. Add the cashews, egg, cornstarch, soy sauce, Peking sauce, and sesame oil to the bowl. Mix well.

2 Lay the wonton wrappers out on a chopping board and spoon small quantities of the mixture into the center of each. Gather the wrapper around the filling at the top, to make little parcels, leaving the top open.

3 Heat the oil for deep-frying in a preheated wok or large, heavy-based pan to 350°F/180°C, or until a cube of bread browns in 30 seconds. Cook the wontons, in batches, for 1–2 minutes, or until golden brown. Drain on paper towels and keep warm while cooking the remaining wontons.

4 Sprinkle the sesame seeds over the wontons. Serve the vegetable dim sum with a soy or plum dipping sauce.

NUTRITION

Calories *295*; Sugars *1 g*; Protein *5 g*;
Carbohydrate *20 g*; Fat *22 g*; Saturates *6 g*

moderate

15 mins

15 mins

🄲 COOK'S TIP

If preferred, arrange the wontons on a heatproof plate and then cook in a steamer for 5–7 minutes for a healthier cooking method.

The Chinese are known for their colorful, crisp vegetables, quickly stir-fried. In this recipe, they are tossed in a tasty soy and Peking sauce.

Chinese Fried Vegetables

1 Heat the peanut oil in a preheated wok or large, heavy-based skillet until it is almost smoking.

2 Add the broccoli florets, ginger, onions, and celery to the wok and cook for 1 minute.

3 Add the spinach, snow peas, scallions, and garlic and cook for 3–4 minutes.

4 Mix together the soy sauce, superfine sugar, sherry, Peking sauce, and vegetable bouillon.

5 Pour the bouillon mixture into the wok, mixing well to coat the vegetables.

6 Cover the wok and cook over a medium heat for 2–3 minutes, or until the vegetables are cooked through, but still crisp.

7 Transfer the vegetables to a warm serving dish and serve immediately.

SERVES 4

2 tbsp peanut oil
12 oz/350 g broccoli florets
1 tbsp chopped fresh gingerroot
2 onions, each cut into 4 pieces
3 celery stalks, sliced
6 oz/175 g baby spinach leaves
$4\frac{1}{2}$ oz/125 g snow peas
6 scallions, quartered
2 garlic cloves, crushed
2 tbsp light soy sauce
2 tsp superfine sugar
2 tbsp dry sherry
1 tbsp Peking sauce
$\frac{2}{3}$ cup vegetable bouillon

NUTRITION
Calories *137*; Sugars *7 g*; Protein *8 g*;
Carbohydrate *10 g*; Fat *7 g*; Saturates *11 g*

easy
5 mins
10 mins

COOK'S TIP

You could use this mixture to fill Chinese crêpes. They are available from Chinese food stores and can be reheated in a steamer in 2–3 minutes.

A mixture of mushrooms common in Western cooking have been used in this recipe for a richly flavored dish.

Spicy Mushrooms

SERVES 4

2 tbsp peanut oil
2 garlic cloves, crushed
3 scallions, chopped
10½ oz/300 g white mushrooms
2 large, open-cap mushrooms, sliced
4½ oz/125 g oyster mushrooms
1 tsp chili sauce
1 tbsp dark soy sauce
1 tbsp Peking sauce
1 tbsp wine vinegar
½ tsp ground Szechuan pepper
1 tbsp dark brown sugar
1 tsp sesame oil
chopped fresh parsley, to garnish

1 Heat the peanut oil in a preheated wok or large, heavy-based skillet until almost smoking.

2 Reduce the heat slightly, add the garlic and scallions to the wok and cook for 30 seconds.

3 Add the mushrooms to the wok with the chili sauce, dark soy sauce, Peking sauce, wine vinegar, ground Szechuan pepper, and dark brown sugar, and cook for 4–5 minutes, or until the mushrooms are cooked through. Stir constantly to prevent the mixture sticking to the bottom of the wok.

4 Sprinkle the sesame oil on top of the mixture in the wok. Transfer to a warm serving dish, garnish with parsley and serve immediately.

NUTRITION
Calories 103; Sugars 4 g; Protein 3 g;
Carbohydrate 5 g; Fat 8 g;Saturates 2 g

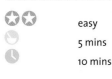

easy
5 mins
10 mins

(👨‍🍳) **COOK'S TIP**

If Chinese dried mushrooms are available, add a small quantity to this dish for texture. Wood ears are available dried from Chinese food stores. They should be rinsed, soaked in hot water for 20 minutes and rinsed again before use.

Bean curd is available in different forms from both Chinese and Western food stores. Firm bean curd is used in this recipe.

Bean Curd *and* Vegetables

1 Heat the oil in a preheated wok or large, heavy-based skillet until almost smoking. Reduce the heat, add the bean curd and cook until golden brown. Remove from the wok with a slotted spoon and drain on paper towels.

2 Pour all but 2 tablespoons of the oil from the wok and return it to the heat. Add the leek, corn cobs, snow peas, red bell pepper, and bamboo shoots and cook for 2–3 minutes.

3 Add the Chinese rice wine, oyster sauce, soy sauce, sugar, salt, and bouillon to the wok and bring to a boil. Blend the cornstarch with the water to form a smooth paste and stir it into the sauce. Return the sauce to a boil and cook, stirring constantly, until thickened and clear.

4 Stir the cooked bean curd into the mixture in the wok and cook for about 1 minute, until hot. Serve immediately.

S E R V E S   4

²/₃ cup vegetable oil

1 lb/450 g firm bean curd, cut into
   1-inch/2.5-cm cubes

1 leek, sliced

4 baby corn cobs, halved lengthwise

2 oz/55 g snow peas

1 red bell pepper, seeded and diced

2 oz/55 g canned bamboo shoots,
   drained and rinsed

1 tbsp Chinese rice wine or dry sherry

4 tbsp oyster sauce

3 tsp light soy sauce

2 tsp superfine sugar

salt

scant ¼ cup vegetable bouillon

1 tsp cornstarch

2 tsp water

N U T R I T I O N
Calories *367*; Sugars *5 g*; Protein *13 g*;
Carbohydrate *11 g*; Fat *30 g*; Saturates *4 g*

⭐⭐   easy

🕐   10 mins

🕐   15 mins

👨‍🍳 **C O O K ' S   T I P**

Bean curd is relatively bland, but it readily absorbs stronger flavors.

Vegan *and* Vegetarian

As vegetables are so plentiful and diverse in the Far East, they play a major role in the diet. Other ingredients, such as bean curd and quorn, are also added to the vegetarian diet, which is both a healthy and an economical choice. Bean curd is produced from the soybean, which is grown in abundance in these countries. The cake variety of bean curd is frequently used in stir-frying for texture and it is perfect for absorbing all of the flavors of the dish. It is also an ideal ingredient for the vegan cook.

The wok is perfect for cooking vegetables as it cooks them very quickly, which helps to retain their nutrients and crispness. This produces a range of colorful and flavorsome recipes, which display the wonderful versatility of all the different kinds of vegetables.

This is a sweet and spicy dish, with the addition of mango chutney and chiles giving a really wonderful combination of flavors.

Spiced Eggplant

SERVES 4

3 tbsp peanut oil
2 onions, sliced
2 garlic cloves, chopped
2 eggplants, diced
2 fresh red chiles, seeded and very finely chopped
2 tbsp raw brown sugar
6 scallions, sliced
3 tbsp mango chutney
oil, for deep-frying
2 garlic cloves, sliced, to garnish

1 Heat the peanut oil in a preheated wok or large, heavy-based skillet, swirling the oil around the bottom of the wok until it is really hot.

2 Add the onions and garlic to the wok, stirring well.

3 Add the eggplant and chiles to the wok and cook for 5 minutes.

4 Add the raw brown sugar, scallions, and mango chutney to the wok, stirring well, and bring to a boil.

5 Reduce the heat, cover, and let simmer, stirring occasionally, for 15 minutes, or until the eggplant is tender.

6 Transfer the stir-fry to serving bowls and keep warm.

7 Heat the oil for deep-frying in the wok and briefly cook the slices of garlic until they brown slightly. Garnish the stir-fry with the deep-fried garlic and serve immediately.

NUTRITION
Calories 208; Sugars 17 g; Protein 1 g;
Carbohydrate 17 g; Fat 15 g; Saturates 2 g

easy

5 mins

25 mins

🍲 **COOK'S TIP**

Chiles vary enormously in their level of heat, so always use with caution, but as a general guide, the smaller the chile the hotter it will be. The seeds are the hottest part and so are usually removed and discarded for a milder flavor.

These small corn balls have a delicious hot and sweet flavor, offset by the aromatic cilantro.

Deep-Fried Chili Corn Balls

1 In a large bowl, mix together the scallions, cilantro, corn, chili powder, chili sauce, coconut, egg, and cornmeal until well blended.

2 Cover the bowl with plastic wrap and let stand for about 10 minutes.

3 Heat the oil for deep-frying in a preheated wok or large, heavy-based pan to 350°F/180°C, or until a cube of bread browns in 30 seconds.

4 Carefully drop spoonfuls of the chili and cornmeal mixture into the hot oil. Deep-fry the chili corn balls, in batches, for 4–5 minutes, or until crispy and a deep golden-brown color.

5 Remove the chili corn balls with a slotted spoon, transfer to paper towels and let drain thoroughly.

6 Transfer the chili corn balls to serving plates and serve with a sweet chili sauce for dipping.

SERVES 4

6 scallions, sliced
3 tbsp chopped fresh cilantro
8 oz/225 g canned corn kernels
1 tsp mild ground chili
1 tbsp sweet chili sauce
1/4 cup shredded coconut
1 egg
1/3 cup cornmeal
oil, for deep-frying
sweet chili sauce, to serve

NUTRITION
Calories *248*; Sugars *6 g*; Protein *6 g*;
Carbohydrate *30 g*; Fat *12 g*; Saturates *5 g*

easy

15 mins

30 mins

COOK'S TIP

For safe deep-frying in a round-bottomed wok, place it on a wok rack so that it rests securely. Only half-fill the wok with oil. Never leave the wok unattended over a high heat.

Butternut squash is, as its name suggests, deliciously buttery and nutty in flavor. If the squash is not in season, use sweet potatoes instead.

Butternut Squash Stir-Fry

SERVES 4

3 tbsp peanut oil
2 lb 4 oz/1 kg butternut squash, seeded and cubed
1 onion, sliced
2 garlic cloves, crushed
1 tsp coriander seeds
1 tsp cumin seeds
2 tbsp chopped fresh cilantro
generous ⅓ cup coconut milk
½ cup water
⅔ cup salted cashews

to garnish
freshly grated lime zest
chopped fresh cilantro
lime wedges

1 Heat the peanut oil in a preheated wok or large, heavy-based skillet.

2 Add the butternut squash, onion, and garlic to the wok and cook for 5 minutes.

3 Stir in the coriander seeds, cumin seeds, and fresh cilantro and cook for 1 minute.

4 Add the coconut milk and water to the wok and bring to a boil. Reduce the heat, cover and let simmer for 10–15 minutes, or until the squash is tender.

5 Add the cashews and stir to combine.

6 Transfer to warm serving dishes and garnish with freshly grated lime zest, fresh cilantro, and lime wedges. Serve hot.

NUTRITION
Calories *301*; Sugars *4 g*; Protein *9 g*;
Carbohydrate *19 g*; Fat *22 g*; Saturates *4 g*

easy

5 mins

25 mins

🍳 **COOK'S TIP**

If you do not have coconut milk, grate some creamed coconut into the dish with the water in step 4.

This is a simple side dish, which is an deal accompaniment to vegetarian entrée dishes.

Leeks *with* Yellow Bean Sauce

1 Heat the peanut oil in a preheated wok or large, heavy-based skillet until smoking.

2 Add the leeks, Napa cabbage, and baby corn cobs to the wok.

3 Cook the vegetables over a high heat for about 5 minutes, or until the edges of the vegetables are slightly brown.

4 Add the scallions to the wok, stirring to combine.

5 Add the yellow bean sauce to the wok. Cook the mixture in the wok for another 2 minutes, or until heated through and the vegetables are thoroughly coated in the sauce.

6 Transfer the vegetables and sauce to warm serving dishes.

SERVES 4

3 tbsp peanut oil
1 lb/450 g leeks, sliced thinly
8 oz/225 g Napa cabbage, shredded
6 oz/175 g baby corn cobs, halved lengthwise
6 scallions, sliced diagonally
4 tbsp yellow bean sauce

NUTRITION
Calories *131*; Sugars *3 g*; Protein *6 g*;
Carbohydrate *7 g*; Fat *9 g*; Saturates *2 g*

⊗⊗   easy
◔   5 mins
🕐   10 mins

🍳 **COOK'S TIP**

Yellow bean sauce adds an authentic Chinese flavor to stir-fries. It is made from crushed salted soybeans mixed with flour and spices to make a thick paste. It is mild in flavor and is excellent with a range of vegetables.

Plum sauce is readily available in jars and has a terrific, sweet flavor, which complements most types of vegetable.

Bok Choy *with* Cashews

SERVES 4

2 tbsp peanut oil
2 red onions, cut into thin wedges
6 oz/175 g red cabbage, shredded
8 oz/225 g bok choy, leaves separated
2 tbsp plum sauce
2/3 cup roasted cashews

1 Heat the peanut oil in a preheated wok or large, heavy-based skillet until it is really hot.

2 Add the onions to the wok and cook for about 5 minutes, or until they just begin to brown.

3 Add the red cabbage to the wok and cook for another 2–3 minutes.

4 Add the bok choy leaves to the wok and cook for about 5 minutes, or until the leaves have just wilted.

5 Drizzle the plum sauce over the vegetables, toss together until well combined and heat until the liquid is bubbling.

6 Scatter with the roasted cashews and transfer to warm serving bowls.

NUTRITION
Calories *241*; Sugars *7 g*; Protein *7 g*;
Carbohydrate *11 g*; Fat *19 g*; Saturates *4 g*

very easy

5 mins

15 mins

COOK'S TIP

Use unsalted peanuts instead of the cashews, if you prefer.

These zucchini fritters are irresistible and could be served as an appetizer or snack with a chili dip.

Deep-Fried Zucchini

1 Lightly whip the egg white until foamy, using a fork.

2 Mix together the cornstarch, salt, and Chinese five-spice and sprinkle onto a large plate.

3 Heat the oil for deep-frying in a preheated wok or large, heavy-based pan.

4 Dip each piece of zucchini into the beaten egg white, then coat in the cornstarch and five-spice mixture.

5 Deep-fry the zucchini, in batches, for about 5 minutes, or until pale golden and crispy. Repeat with the remaining zucchini.

6 Remove the zucchini with a slotted spoon and let drain on paper towels while deep-frying the remainder.

7 Transfer the zucchini to warmed serving plates and serve immediately with a chili dip.

SERVES 4

1 egg white
1/3 cup cornstarch
1 tsp salt
1 tsp ground Chinese five-spice
oil, for deep-frying
1 lb/450 g zucchini, sliced into sticks or rounds
chili dip, to serve

NUTRITION
Calories 117; Sugars 2 g; Protein 3 g; Carbohydrate 14 g; Fat 6 g; Saturates 1 g

⭐ very easy
🕐 5 mins
🕐 20 mins

🍳 **COOK'S TIP**

Alter the seasoning by using ground chili or curry powder instead of the Chinese five-spice, if you prefer.

This stir-fry is the perfect accompaniment to bean curd dishes, and it is so quick and simple to make.

Honey-Fried Spinach

SERVES 4

3 tbsp peanut oil
12 oz/350 g shiitake mushrooms, sliced
2 garlic cloves, crushed
12 oz/350 g baby spinach leaves
2 tbsp dry sherry
2 tbsp clear honey
4 scallions, sliced

1 Heat the peanut oil in a preheated wok or large, heavy-based skillet.

2 Add the shiitake mushrooms to the wok and cook for about 5 minutes, or until the mushrooms have softened.

3 Stir the garlic and baby spinach leaves into the wok and cook for another 2–3 minutes, or until the spinach leaves have wilted.

4 Mix together the dry sherry and clear honey in a small bowl until well combined. Drizzle the sherry and honey mixture over the spinach and heat through, stirring to coat the spinach leaves thoroughly in the mixture.

5 Transfer the stir-fry to warm serving dishes, scatter with the chopped scallions and serve immediately.

NUTRITION
Calories *146*; Sugars *9 g*; Protein *4 g*; Carbohydrate *10 g*; Fat *9 g*; Saturates *2 g*

easy

5 mins

15 mins

🍳 COOK'S TIP

Single-flower honey has a more individual flavor than blended honey. Acacia honey is typically Chinese, but you could also try clover, lemon blossom, lime flower, or orange blossom honey.

Although sweet and sour flavorings are mainly associated with pork, they are ideal for adding interest to vegetables, as in this tasty recipe.

Sweet *and* Sour Cauliflower

1 Bring a large pan of water to a boil. Add the cauliflower to the pan and cook for 2 minutes. Drain the cauliflower thoroughly.

2 Heat the sunflower oil in a preheated wok or large, heavy-based skillet.

3 Add the onion and carrots to the wok and cook for about 5 minutes.

4 Add the cauliflower and snow peas to the wok and cook for 2–3 minutes.

5 Add the mango and beansprouts to the wok and cook for about 2 minutes.

6 Mix together the cilantro, lime juice, honey, and coconut milk in a bowl.

7 Add the cilantro and coconut mixture to the wok and cook for about 2 minutes, or until the juices are bubbling.

8 Transfer the cauliflower stir-fry to serving dishes and serve immediately.

SERVES 4

1 lb/450 g cauliflower florets
2 tbsp sunflower oil
1 onion, sliced
8 oz/225 g carrots, sliced
3½ oz/100 g snow peas
1 ripe mango, peeled, pitted and sliced
1 cup beansprouts
3 tbsp chopped fresh cilantro
3 tbsp fresh lime juice
1 tbsp clear honey
6 tbsp coconut milk

NUTRITION
Calories *154*; Sugars *16 g*; Protein *6 g*; Carbohydrate *17 g*; Fat *7 g*; Saturates *1 g*

COOK'S TIP

You could use broccoli instead of the cauliflower, if preferred.

easy

5 mins

15 mins

This quick dish is an ideal lunchtime meal, packed with mixed mushrooms in a sweet sauce.

Stir-Fried Japanese Noodles

SERVES 4

8 oz/225 g Japanese egg noodles
2 tbsp sunflower oil
1 red onion, sliced
1 garlic clove, crushed
1 lb/450 g mixed mushrooms (shiitake, oyster, brown cap)
12 oz/350 g bok choy, leaves separated
2 tbsp sweet sherry
6 tbsp oyster sauce
4 scallions, sliced
1 tbsp toasted sesame seeds

1 Place the Japanese egg noodles in a large bowl. Pour enough boiling water over to cover and let the noodles soak for 10 minutes.

2 Heat the sunflower oil in a preheated wok or large, heavy-based skillet.

3 Add the red onion and garlic to the wok and cook for 2–3 minutes, or until softened.

4 Add the mushrooms to the wok and cook for about 5 minutes, or until they have softened.

5 Drain the egg noodles thoroughly.

6 Add the the bok choy, noodles, sweet sherry, and oyster sauce to the wok. Toss the ingredients together and cook for 2–3 minutes, or until the liquid is just bubbling.

7 Transfer the mushroom noodles to warm serving bowls and scatter with scallions and toasted sesame seeds. Serve immediately.

NUTRITION

Calories *379*; Sugars *8 g*; Protein *12 g*; Carbohydrate *53 g*; Fat *13 g*; Saturates *3 g*

easy

15 mins

15 mins

COOK'S TIP

The variety of mushrooms in large food stores has improved and a good mixture should be easily obtainable. If not, use the more common white and flat mushrooms.

Bean curd is ideal for absorbing the other flavors in this dish. If marinated bean curd is used, it will add a flavor of its own.

Bean Curd Casserole

1 Heat the peanut oil in a preheated wok or large, heavy-based skillet.

2 Add the scallions, celery, broccoli, zucchini, garlic, spinach, and bean curd to the wok and cook for 3–4 minutes.

3 To make the sauce, mix together all the ingredients in a flameproof casserole and bring to a boil.

4 Add the stir-fried vegetables and bean curd to the casserole, reduce the heat, then cover, and let simmer for 10 minutes.

5 Transfer the bean curd and vegetables to a warm serving dish and serve with boiled white rice.

SERVES 4

2 tbsp peanut oil
8 scallions, cut into batons
2 celery stalks, sliced
4½ oz/125 g broccoli florets
4½ oz/125 g zucchini, sliced
2 garlic cloves, sliced thinly
1 lb/450 g baby spinach leaves
1 lb/450 g firm bean curd, cut into
    1-inch/2.5-cm cubes
boiled white rice, to serve

sauce

scant 2 cups vegetable bouillon
2 tbsp light soy sauce
3 tbsp Peking sauce
½ tsp ground chili
1 tbsp sesame oil

NUTRITION
Calories *228*; Sugars *3 g*; Protein *16 g*;
Carbohydrate *7 g*; Fat *15 g*; Saturates *2 g*

easy

5 mins

15 mins

COOK'S TIP

This recipe incorporates mainly green vegetables, but you could alter them according to likes and dislikes. Add mushrooms, carrots, baby corn, or Chinese leaves, if preferred.

Sweet-and-sour was one of the first Chinese sauces introduced to the West, and remains one of the most popular.

Sweet *and* Sour Bean Curd

SERVES 4

2 tbsp vegetable oil
2 garlic cloves, crushed
2 celery stalks, sliced thinly
1 carrot, cut into thin strips
1 green bell pepper, seeded and diced
$2^3/_4$ oz/75 g snow peas, halved diagonally
8 baby corn cobs
$4^1/_2$ oz/125 g beansprouts
1 lb/450 g firm bean curd, cubed
boiled rice or noodles, to serve

sauce

2 tbsp light brown sugar
2 tbsp rice wine vinegar
1 cup vegetable bouillon
1 tsp tomato paste
1 tbsp cornstarch

1 Heat the vegetable oil in a preheated wok or large, heavy-based skillet until it is almost smoking. Reduce the heat slightly, add the garlic, celery, carrot, green bell pepper, snow peas, and corn cobs and cook for 3–4 minutes.

2 Add the beansprouts and bean curd to the wok and cook for another 2 minutes, stirring well.

3 To make the sauce, combine the sugar, wine vinegar, bouillon, tomato paste, and cornstarch, stirring well to mix. Stir into the wok, bring to a boil and cook, stirring, until the sauce thickens and clears. Continue to cook for 1 minute. Serve the bean curd with boiled rice or noodles.

NUTRITION

Calories *205*; Sugars *12 g*; Protein *11 g*; Carbohydrate *17 g*; Fat *11 g*; Saturates *1 g*

easy

5 mins

10 mins

🍴 COOK'S TIP

Be careful not to break up the fragile cubes of bean curd when stirring.

This tasty rice dish can either be served as an entrée or as an accompaniment to other vegetable recipes.

Chinese Vegetable Rice

1 Place the rice and turmeric in a pan of lightly salted water and bring to a boil. Reduce the heat and let simmer until the rice is just tender. Drain the rice thoroughly. Set aside until required.

2 Heat the sunflower oil in a preheated wok or large, heavy-based skillet.

3 Add the zucchini to the wok and cook for about 2 minutes.

4 Add the red and green bell peppers and chile to the wok and cook for 2–3 minutes.

5 Add the cooked rice to the mixture in the wok, a little at a time, tossing well after each addition.

6 Add the carrots, beansprouts, and scallions to the wok and cook for another 2 minutes.

7 Drizzle the soy sauce over the stir-fry and serve at once, garnished with extra scallions, if desired.

SERVES 4

1¾ cups long-grain white rice
1 tsp turmeric
2 tbsp sunflower oil
8 oz/225 g zucchini, sliced
1 red bell pepper, seeded and sliced
1 green bell pepper, seeded and sliced
1 fresh green chile, seeded and finely chopped
1 medium carrot, grated coarsely
1½ cups beansprouts
6 scallions, sliced, plus extra to garnish (optional)
2 tbsp soy sauce
salt

NUTRITION
Calories 140; Sugars 3 g; Protein 3 g; Carbohydrate 20 g; Fat 17 g; Saturates 1 g

⭐⭐⭐   moderate
🕐   5 mins
🕐   25 mins

👨‍🍳 COOK'S TIP

For real luxury, add a few saffron strands infused in boiling water instead of the turmeric.

This spicy vegetable stir-fry has rice added to it and can be served as a substantial entrée.

Vegetables *with* Hoisin

SERVES 4

2 tbsp sunflower oil
1 red onion, sliced thinly
1 carrot, sliced thinly
1 yellow bell pepper, seeded and diced
1 cup cooked brown rice
6 oz/175 g snow peas
1¾ cups beansprouts
4 tbsp Peking sauce
1 tbsp snipped fresh chives

1 Heat the sunflower oil in a preheated wok or large, heavy-based skillet.

2 Add the red onion, carrots, and yellow bell pepper to the wok and cook for about 3 minutes.

3 Add the cooked brown rice, snow peas, and beansprouts to the mixture in the wok and cook for another 2 minutes. Stir briskly to ensure that the ingredients are well mixed and the rice grains are separated.

4 Stir the Peking sauce into the vegetables and mix well until combined and completely heated through.

5 Transfer the vegetable stir-fry to warm serving dishes and scatter with the snipped fresh chives. Serve immediately.

NUTRITION
Calories 120; Sugars 6 g; Protein 4 g;
Carbohydrate 12 g; Fat 6 g; Saturates 1 g

easy
10 mins
10 mins

COOK'S TIP

Peking sauce is a dark, reddish-brown sauce made from soy beans, garlic, chili, and various other spices, and is commonly used in Chinese cookery. It may also be used as a dipping sauce.

This is a crunchy and colorful stir-fry, topped with crisp, shredded leeks for both flavor and color.

Bell Peppers *and* Chestnuts

1 Heat the oil for deep-frying in a wok or large, heavy-based skillet.

2 Add the leeks to the wok and cook for 2–3 minutes, or until crispy. Remove with a slotted spoon and drain on paper towels. Set aside until required.

3 Heat the peanut oil in the wok. Add the yellow, green, and red bell peppers to the wok and cook over a high heat for about 5 minutes, or until they begin to brown at the edges and have softened.

4 Add the water chestnuts, garlic, and light soy sauce to the wok and cook the vegetables for another 2–3 minutes.

5 Spoon the bell pepper stir-fry on to warm serving plates, garnish with the crispy leeks and serve.

SERVES 4

oil, for deep-frying
8 oz/225 g leeks, shredded
3 tbsp peanut oil
1 yellow bell pepper, seeded and diced
1 green bell pepper, seeded and diced
1 red bell pepper, seeded and diced
7 oz/200 g canned water chestnuts, drained and sliced
2 garlic cloves, crushed
3 tbsp light soy sauce

NUTRITION
Calories *192*; Sugars *5 g*; Protein *3 g*; Carbohydrate *13 g*; Fat *14 g*; Saturates *13 g*

✪✪   easy

◔   5 mins

🕐   15 mins

 COOK'S TIP

Add 1 tablespoon of Peking sauce with the soy sauce in step 4 for a richer flavor and extra spice.

Known as Gado Gado in Indonesia, this is a true classic which never fades in popularity. The delicious warm salad is topped with quarters of hard-boiled egg and served with a peanut sauce.

Vegetable Stir-Fry *with* Eggs

SERVES 4

2 eggs
2 tbsp vegetable oil
3 small carrots, grated coarsely
12 oz/350 g white cabbage, shredded
1 red bell pepper, seeded and sliced thinly
1½ cups beansprouts
1 tbsp tomato catsup
2 tbsp soy sauce
½ cup salted peanuts, chopped
peanut sauce, to serve

1 Bring a small pan of water to a boil. Add the eggs to the pan and cook for about 7 minutes. Remove the eggs from the pan and let cool under cold running water for 1 minute. Peel the eggs and cut into quarters.

2 Heat the vegetable oil in a preheated wok or large, heavy-based skillet.

3 Add the carrots, white cabbage, and red bell pepper to the wok and cook for 3 minutes.

4 Add the beansprouts to the wok and cook for 2 minutes.

5 Combine the tomato catsup and soy sauce in a small bowl and add to the vegetables in the wok .

6 Add the chopped peanuts to the wok and cook for 1 minute.

7 Transfer the stir-fry to warm serving plates and garnish with the hard-cooked egg quarters. Serve with a peanut sauce.

NUTRITION
Calories 269; Sugars 12 g; Protein 12 g;
Carbohydrate 14 g; Fat 19 g; Saturates 3 g

easy

10 mins

15 mins

🍳 **COOK'S TIP**

The eggs are cooled in cold water after cooking in order to prevent the egg yolk turning black around the edges.

This recipe, as the title suggests, is a colorful mixture of eight vegetables, cooked in a black bean and soy sauce.

Eight Jewel Vegetables

1 Heat the peanut oil in a preheated wok or large, heavy-based skillet until it is almost smoking.

2 Reduce the heat slightly, add the scallions and garlic and cook for about 30 seconds.

3 Add the green and red bell peppers, red chile, water chestnuts, and zucchini to the wok and cook for 2–3 minutes, or until the vegetables begin to soften.

4 Add the oyster mushrooms, black bean sauce, Chinese rice wine, dark soy sauce, dark brown sugar and water to the wok and cook for another 4 minutes.

5 Sprinkle the stir-fry with sesame oil and serve immediately.

SERVES 4

2 tbsp peanut oil
6 scallions, sliced
3 garlic cloves, crushed
1 green bell pepper, seeded and diced
1 red bell pepper, seeded and diced
1 fresh red chile, sliced
2 tbsp chopped water chestnuts
1 zucchini, chopped
$4\frac{1}{2}$ oz/125 g oyster mushrooms
3 tbsp black bean sauce
2 tsp Chinese rice wine or dry sherry
4 tbsp dark soy sauce
1 tsp dark brown sugar
2 tbsp water
1 tsp sesame oil

NUTRITION
Calories *110*; Sugars *3 g*; Protein *4 g*;
Carbohydrate *7 g*; Fat *8 g*; Saturates *1 g*

easy
5 mins
10 mins

COOK'S TIP

Eight jewels or treasures form a traditional part of the Chinese New Year celebrations. The Kitchen God, an important figure, is sent to give a report to heaven, returning on New Year's Eve in time for the feasting.

Marinated bean curd is ideal in this recipe for added flavor, although the spicy coating is very tasty with plain bean curd.

Spicy Fried Bean Curd Triangles

SERVES 4

1 tbsp sea salt
4½ tsp ground Chinese five-spice
3 tbsp light brown sugar
2 garlic cloves, crushed
1 tsp grated fresh gingerroot
1lb/450 g firm bean curd
vegetable oil, for deep-frying
2 leeks, shredded and halved, plus extra to garnish

1 Mix together the salt, Chinese five-spice, sugar, garlic, and ginger in a bowl and transfer to a plate.

2 Cut the bean curd cakes in half diagonally to form 2 triangles. Cut each triangle in half and then in half again to form 16 triangles. Roll the bean curd in the spice mixture, turning to coat thoroughly. Set aside for 1 hour.

3 Heat the vegetable oil for deep-frying in a preheated wok or large, heavy-based pan until it is almost smoking.

4 Reduce the heat slightly, add the bean curd triangles and fry for 5 minutes, until golden brown. Remove the bean curd from the wok with a slotted spoon, set aside and keep warm until required.

5 Add the leeks to the wok and cook for 1 minute. Remove from the wok and drain on paper towels.

6 Arrange the leeks on a warm serving plate and place the fried bean curd on top. Garnish with the fresh shredded leek and serve immediately.

NUTRITION
Calories 224; Sugars 17 g; Protein 10 g;
Carbohydrate 18 g; Fat 13 g; Saturates 2 g

★★★ moderate
1 hr 15 mins
20 mins

 COOK'S TIP

Cook the bean curd in batches and keep each batch warm until all of the bean curd has been cooked and is ready to serve.

This dish tastes as fresh as it looks. Try to get hold of baby vegetables as they look and taste so much better in this dish.

Cantonese Garden Vegetables

1 Heat the peanut oil in a preheated wok or large, heavy-based skillet until it is almost smoking.

2 Add the Chinese five-spice, carrots, celery, leeks, snow peas, zucchini, and corn cobs and cook for 3–4 minutes.

3 Add the bean curd to the wok and cook for a further 2 minutes, stirring gently so the bean curd does not break up.

4 Stir the fresh orange juice and clear honey into the wok, reduce the heat and cook for 1–2 minutes.

5 Transfer the stir-fry to a serving dish, garnish with celery leaves and orange zest and serve with boiled rice or noodles.

SERVES 4

2 tbsp peanut oil
1 tsp ground Chinese five-spice
2¾ oz/75 g baby carrots, halved
2 celery stalks, sliced
2 baby leeks, sliced
1¾ oz/50 g snow peas
4 baby zucchini, halved lengthwise
8 baby corn cobs
8 oz/225 g firm marinated bean curd, cubed
4 tbsp fresh orange juice
1 tbsp clear honey
boiled rice or noodles, to serve

to garnish
celery leaves
finely grated orange zest

NUTRITION
Calories *130*; Sugars *8 g*; Protein *6 g*;
Carbohydrate *8 g*; Fat *8 g*; Saturates *1 g*

easy

5 mins

10 mins

⊕ COOK'S TIP

Lemon juice is just as delicious as the orange juice in this stir-fry. Use 3 tablespoons of lemon juice instead of 4 tablespoons of orange juice.

Rice *and* Noodles

Rice and noodles are staples in the Far East, as they are cheap, plentiful, nutritious, and delicious. They are extremely versatile ingredients and are therefore always served as part of a meal. Many rice and noodle dishes are served as accompaniments and others as main dishes combined with meat, vegetables, and fish, all flavored with fragrant spices and seasonings.

Plain rice is served to punctuate a large meal and help settle the stomach between rich, spicy courses. Noodles vary from country to country and are eaten in various forms. Thin egg noodles are made from wheat flour, water, and egg and are probably the most common in the Western diet. Available fresh or dried, they require very little cooking and are perfect for quick and easy meals.

This rice dish is really colorful and crunchy with the addition of corn and red kidney beans.

Fried Rice *with* Spicy Beans

SERVES 4

3 tbsp sunflower oil
1 onion, chopped finely
scant 1¼ cups long-grain white rice
1 green bell pepper, seeded and diced
1 tsp ground chili
2½ cups boiling water
3½ oz/100 g canned corn kernels, drained
8 oz/225 g canned red kidney beans, drained and rinsed
2 tbsp chopped fresh cilantro, plus extra, to garnish (optional)

1 Heat the sunflower oil in a preheated wok or large, heavy-based skillet.

2 Add the onion to the wok and cook for about 2 minutes, or until softened.

3 Add the rice, green bell pepper, and chili powder to the wok and cook for 1 minute.

4 Pour the boiling water into the wok. Bring back to a boil, then reduce the heat and let the mixture simmer for 15 minutes, until the water has been absorbed and the rice is tender.

5 Add the corn, kidney beans, and cilantro to the wok and heat through, stirring occasionally.

6 Transfer to a serving bowl and serve hot, scattered with extra fresh cilantro, if desired.

NUTRITION
Calories *374*; Sugars *6 g*; Protein *9 g*;
Carbohydrate *64 g*; Fat *9 g*; Saturates *1 g*

easy

5 mins

25 mins

COOK'S TIP

For extra heat, add 1 chopped fresh red chile with the ground chili in step 3.

This fragrant, sweet rice is delicious served with meat, vegetable, or fish dishes as part of a Chinese menu.

Fragrant Coconut Rice

1 Rinse the rice thoroughly under cold running water until the water runs completely clear.

2 Drain the rice thoroughly in a strainer set over a large bowl. (This is to remove some of the starch and to prevent the grains from sticking together.)

3 Place the rice in a wok or pan with the water.

4 Add the salt and coconut milk to the wok and bring to a boil.

5 Cover the wok with a lid or make a lid of foil, curved into a domed shape and resting on the sides. Reduce the heat and let simmer for 10 minutes.

6 Remove the lid from the wok and fluff up the rice with a fork—all of the liquid should be absorbed and the rice grains should be tender. If not, add more water and continue to simmer for a few more minutes until all of the liquid has been absorbed.

7 Spoon the rice into a warm serving bowl and scatter with the shredded coconut. Serve immediately.

COOK'S TIP

Coconut milk is not the liquid found inside coconuts—that is called coconut water. Coconut milk is made from the white coconut flesh soaked in water and milk and then squeezed to extract all the flavor.

SERVES 4

1$\frac{1}{3}$ cups long-grain white rice
2$\frac{1}{2}$ cups water
$\frac{1}{2}$ tsp salt
generous $\frac{1}{3}$ cup coconut milk
$\frac{1}{4}$ cup shredded coconut

NUTRITION
Calories *306*; Sugars *2 g*; Protein *5 g*; Carbohydrate *61 g*; Fat *6 g*; Saturates *4 g*

very easy

5 mins

15 mins

In this classic Chinese dish, boiled rice is cooked with peas, scallions, and egg, and flavored with soy sauce.

Egg Fried Rice

SERVES 4

¾ cup long-grain rice
3 eggs, beaten
2 tbsp vegetable oil
2 garlic cloves, crushed
4 scallions, chopped
1 cup cooked peas
1 tbsp light soy sauce
pinch of salt
shredded scallion, to garnish

1 Cook the rice in a pan of boiling water for 10–12 minutes, until almost cooked, but not soft. Drain the rice well, rinse under cold running water and drain thoroughly again. Set aside to cool.

2 Place the beaten eggs in a pan and cook over a gentle heat, stirring until softly scrambled.

3 Heat the vegetable oil in a preheated wok or large, heavy-based skillet, swirling the oil around the bottom of the wok until it is really hot.

4 Add the garlic, scallions, and peas and stir-fry, for 1–2 minutes. Stir the rice into the wok, mixing to combine.

5 Add the eggs, light soy sauce, and a pinch of salt to the wok and stir to mix in the egg thoroughly.

6 Transfer the egg fried rice to serving dishes and serve garnished with the shredded scallion.

NUTRITION
Calories *203*; Sugars *1 g*; Protein *9 g*;
Carbohydrate *19 g*; Fat *11 g*; Saturates *2 g*

easy
10 mins
20 mins

COOK'S TIP

The rice is rinsed under cold water to wash out the starch and to prevent the grains from sticking together.

This dish can be served as an accompaniment or as a vegetarian entrée in itself.

Vegetable Fried Rice

1 Cook the rice in a pan of boiling water for 15 minutes, until tender. Drain the rice well, rinse under cold running water and drain thoroughly again. Set aside to cool.

2 Heat the peanut oil in a preheated wok or large, heavy-based skillet. Add the garlic and Chinese five-spice powder and cook for 30 seconds.

3 Add the fine green beans, green bell pepper, and baby corn cobs to the wok, and cook for 2 minutes.

4 Stir the bamboo shoots, tomatoes, peas, and rice into the mixture in the wok and cook for 1 more minute.

5 Sprinkle with sesame oil and transfer to serving dishes. Serve immediately.

SERVES 4

²/₃ cup long-grain white rice
3 tbsp peanut oil
2 garlic cloves, crushed
¹/₂ tsp ground Chinese five-spice
2 oz/55 g fine green beans
1 green bell pepper, seeded and chopped
4 baby corn cobs, sliced lengthwise
1 oz/25 g canned bamboo shoots, drained and chopped
3 tomatoes, skinned, seeded, and chopped
¹/₂ cup cooked peas
1 tsp sesame oil

NUTRITION
Calories 175; Sugars 3 g; Protein 3 g;
Carbohydrate 20 g; Fat 10 g; Saturates 2 g

★★ easy
🕐 10 mins
🕐 20 mins

🍳 **COOK'S TIP**

Use a selection of vegetables of your choice in this recipe, cutting them to a similar size in order to ensure that they cook in the same amount of time.

Spinach is used in this
recipe to give the rice a
wonderful green color.
Tossed with the carrot
strips, it is a really
appealing dish.

Green Fried Rice

SERVES 4

²/₃ cup long-grain white rice
2 tbsp vegetable oil
2 garlic cloves, crushed
1 tsp grated fresh gingerroot
1 carrot, cut into very thin sticks
1 zucchini, diced
8 oz/225 g baby spinach leaves
2 tsp light soy sauce
2 tsp light brown sugar

1 Cook the rice in a pan of boiling water for about 15 minutes, until tender.
Drain well, rinse under cold running water, and drain thoroughly again. Set
aside to cool.

2 Heat the vegetable oil in a preheated wok or large, heavy-based skillet.

3 Add the garlic and ginger to the wok and cook for about 30 seconds.

4 Add the carrot and zucchini to the mixture in the wok and cook for about
2 minutes, until the vegetables have softened, but still retain their crunch.

5 Add the baby spinach leaves and cook for 1 minute, until wilted.

6 Add the rice, soy sauce, and sugar to the wok and mix together well.

7 Transfer the green fried rice to serving dishes and serve immediately.

NUTRITION

Calories 139; Sugars 2 g; Protein 3 g;
Carbohydrate 18 g; Fat 7 g; Saturates 1 g

easy

5 mins

20 mins

🍳 COOK'S TIP

Light soy sauce, as its name suggests, has a lighter flavor than the sweeter,
dark soy sauce, which gives the food a rich, reddish color.

This dish is a popular choice in Chinese restaurants. Ham and shrimp are mixed with vegetables in a soy-flavored rice.

Special Fried Rice

1 Cook the rice in a pan of boiling water for about 15 minutes, until tender. Drain well, rinse under cold running water and drain thoroughly again. Set aside to cool.

2 Heat 1 tablespoon of the vegetable oil in a preheated wok or large, heavy-based skillet.

3 Add the beaten eggs and a further 1 teaspoon of oil. Tilt the wok so that the egg covers the bottom to make a thin omelet.

4 Cook until lightly browned on the underside, then flip the omelet over and cook on the other side for 1 minute. Remove from the wok and let cool.

5 Heat the remaining oil in the wok and cook the garlic and ginger for 30 seconds. Add the scallions, peas, beansprouts, ham, and shrimp, then cook for 2 minutes.

6 Stir in the soy sauce and rice and cook for a further 2 minutes. Transfer the rice to serving dishes. Roll up the omelet, slice it very thinly and use to garnish the rice. Serve immediately.

COOK'S TIP

Since this recipe contains meat and seafood, it is an ideal partner to a simple vegetable dish.

SERVES 4

²⁄₃ cup long-grain white rice
2 tbsp vegetable oil
2 eggs, beaten
2 garlic cloves, crushed
1 tsp grated fresh gingerroot
3 scallions, sliced
³⁄₄ cup cooked peas
1½ cups beansprouts
1⅓ cups shredded ham
5½ oz/150 g peeled, cooked shrimp
2 tbsp light soy sauce

NUTRITION
Calories *301*; Sugars *1 g*; Protein *26 g*;
Carbohydrate *21 g*; Fat *13 g*; Saturates *3 g*

easy

5 mins

25 mins

Canned crabmeat is used in this recipe for convenience, but fresh white crabmeat could be used—quite deliciously—in its place.

Crab Fried Rice

SERVES 4

⅔ cup long-grain white rice
2 tbsp peanut oil
4½ oz/125 g canned white crabmeat, drained
1 leek, sliced
1½ cups beansprouts
2 eggs, beaten
1 tbsp light soy sauce
2 tsp lime juice
1 tsp sesame oil
salt
sliced lime, to garnish

1 Cook the rice in a pan of boiling salted water for 15 minutes, until tender. Drain well, rinse under cold running water and drain thoroughly again. Set aside to cool.

2 Heat the peanut oil in a preheated wok or large, heavy-based skillet until it is really hot.

3 Add the crabmeat, leek, and beansprouts to the wok and cook for 2–3 minutes. Remove the mixture from the wok with a slotted spoon and set aside until required.

4 Add the eggs to the wok and cook, stirring occasionally, for 2–3 minutes, until they begin to set. Stir the rice and crabmeat, leek, and beansprout mixture into the eggs in the wok.

5 Add the soy sauce and lime juice to the mixture in the wok. Cook for 1 minute, stirring to combine, season with salt, and sprinkle with sesame oil.

6 Transfer the crab fried rice to a serving dish, garnish with the sliced lime and serve immediately.

NUTRITION
Calories *225*; Sugars *1 g*; Protein *12 g*;
Carbohydrate *20 g*; Fat *11 g*; Saturates *2 g*

moderate

5 mins

25 mins

COOK'S TIP

Cooked lobster may be used instead of the crab for a really special dish.

This soup-like main course rice dish is packed with fresh seafood and is typically Thai in flavor.

Rice *with* Seafood

1 Discard any mussels with damaged shells or open ones that do not close when firmly tapped. Heat 4 tablespoons of the bouillon in a large pan. Add the mussels, cover and shake the pan until the mussels open. Remove from the heat and discard any mussels which do not open.

2 Heat the oil in a preheated wok or large, heavy-based skillet and cook the garlic, ginger, chile, and scallions for 30 seconds. Add the bouillon and bring to a boil.

3 Stir in the rice, then add the squid, fish, and shrimp. Reduce the heat and let simmer for 15 minutes, or until the rice is cooked. Add the fish sauce and cooked mussels.

4 Ladle into wide bowls and sprinkle with cilantro, before serving.

SERVES 4

12 mussels in their shells, cleaned
8$\frac{3}{4}$ cups fish bouillon
2 tbsp vegetable oil
1 garlic clove, crushed
1 tsp grated fresh gingerroot
1 fresh red bird's-eye chile, chopped
2 scallions, chopped
scant 1$\frac{1}{4}$ cups long-grain white rice
2 small squid, cleaned and sliced
3$\frac{1}{2}$ oz/100 g firm white fish fillet, such as halibut or monkfish, cut into chunks
3$\frac{1}{2}$ oz/100 g peeled, raw shrimp
2 tbsp fish sauce
3 tbsp shredded fresh cilantro

NUTRITION
Calories 370; Sugars 0 g; Protein 27 g; Carbohydrate 52 g; Fat 8 g; Saturates 1 g

⭐⭐⭐   moderate
🕐   10 mins
🕐   25 mins

🍴 **COOK'S TIP**

You could use leftover cooked rice for this dish. Just simmer the seafood gently until cooked, then stir in the rice at the end and heat thoroughly.

This is a really colorful main meal or side dish, which tastes just as good as it looks.

Chinese Chicken Rice

SERVES 4

1¾ cups long-grain white rice
1 tsp turmeric
2 tbsp sunflower oil
12 oz/350 g skinless, boneless chicken breasts or thighs, sliced
1 red bell pepper, seeded and sliced
1 green bell pepper, seeded and sliced
1 fresh green chile, seeded and finely chopped
1 carrot, grated coarsely
1½ cups beansprouts
6 scallions, sliced, plus extra to garnish
2 tbsp soy sauce
salt

1 Place the rice and turmeric in a large pan of lightly salted water and cook for 10 minutes, or until just tender. Drain the rice, rinse under cold running water and drain thoroughly again. Set aside to cool.

2 Heat the sunflower oil in a preheated wok or large, heavy-based skillet.

3 Add the chicken to the wok and cook over a high heat until the chicken just begins to turn a golden color.

4 Add the red and green bell peppers and chile to the wok and cook for 2–3 minutes.

5 Add the cooked rice to the wok, a little at a time, tossing well after each addition until well combined and the grains of rice are separated.

6 Add the carrot, beansprouts, and scallions to the wok and cook for a further 2 minutes.

7 Drizzle the soy sauce over the rice mixture and toss to combine.

8 Transfer the Chinese chicken rice to a warm serving dish, garnish with extra scallions, and serve at once.

NUTRITION
Calories 324; Sugars 4 g; Protein 24 g; Carbohydrate 37 g; Fat 10 g; Saturates 2 g

moderate

10 mins

25 mins

This is a spicy casserole of rice, chicken, and vegetables in a soy and ginger flavored sauce.

Chicken *and* Rice Casserole

1 Cook the rice in a pan of boiling water for about 15 minutes, until tender. Drain well, rinse under cold running water and drain again thoroughly. Set aside to cool.

2 Mix together the sherry, soy sauces, sugar, salt, and sesame oil.

3 Stir the chicken into the soy mixture, turning to coat it. Let the chicken marinate in the refrigerator for about 30 minutes.

4 Bring the bouillon to a boil in a preheated wok or large, heavy-based skillet. Add the chicken with the marinade, mushrooms, water chestnuts, broccoli, yellow bell pepper, and ginger.

5 Stir in the rice, reduce the heat, cover, and cook for 25–30 minutes, until the chicken and vegetables are cooked through. Transfer to serving plates, garnish with chives and serve.

SERVES 4

generous ²/₃ cup long-grain white rice
1 tbsp dry sherry
2 tbsp light soy sauce
2 tbsp dark soy sauce
2 tsp dark brown sugar
1 tsp salt
1 tsp sesame oil
2 lb/900 g skinless, boneless chicken, diced
3½ cups chicken bouillon
2 open-cap mushrooms, sliced
2 oz/60 g canned water chestnuts, drained and halved
2¾ oz/75 g broccoli florets
1 yellow bell pepper, sliced
4 tsp grated fresh gingerroot
whole chives, to garnish

NUTRITION
Calories *502*; Sugars *2 g*; Protein *55 g*; Carbohydrate *52 g*; Fat *9 g*; Saturates *3 g*

✪✪✪   moderate
🕐   35 mins
🕐   50 mins

🍳 **COOK'S TIP**

This dish works equally well with beef or pork. Chinese dried mushrooms may be used, instead of the open-cap mushrooms, if rehydrated in hot water before adding to the dish.

This classic dish requires little introduction as it is already a favorite among most Chinese food enthusiasts.

Chicken Chow Mein

SERVES 4

9 oz/250 g medium egg noodles
2 tbsp sunflower oil
9½ oz/275 g cooked chicken breasts, sliced thinly
1 garlic clove, finely chopped
1 red bell pepper, seeded and sliced thinly
3½ oz/100 g shiitake mushrooms, sliced
6 scallions, sliced
1 cup beansprouts
3 tbsp soy sauce
1 tbsp sesame oil

1 Place the egg noodles in a large bowl or dish and break them up slightly. Pour enough boiling water over the noodles to cover and let stand.

2 Heat the sunflower oil in a preheated wok or large, heavy-based skillet. Add the chicken, garlic, red bell pepper, mushrooms, scallions, and beansprouts to the wok and cook for about 5 minutes.

3 Drain the noodles thoroughly. Add the noodles to the wok, toss well and cook for a further 5 minutes.

4 Drizzle the soy sauce and sesame oil over the noodle mixture in the wok and toss well until combined.

5 Transfer the chicken noodles to warm serving bowls and serve immediately.

NUTRITION
Calories 230; Sugars 2 g; Protein 19 g; Carbohydrate 14 g; Fat 11 g; Saturates 2 g

easy

5 mins

20 mins

COOK'S TIP

You can make the chow mein with a selection of vegetables for a vegetarian dish, if preferred.

This is a variation of egg fried rice, which may be served as an accompaniment to a main meal dish.

Sweet Chili Pork Fried Rice

1 Heat the sunflower oil in a preheated wok or large, heavy-based skillet.

2 Add the pork to the wok and cook for 5 minutes.

3 Add the sweet chili sauce to the wok and allow to bubble, stirring, for 2–3 minutes, or until it becomes syrupy.

4 Add the onion, carrots, zucchini, and bamboo shoots to the wok and cook for another 3 minutes.

5 Add the cooked rice and cook for 2–3 minutes, or until the rice is completely heated through.

6 Drizzle the beaten egg over the top of the fried rice and cook, tossing the stir-fry in the wok with two spoons, until the egg sets.

7 Scatter with fresh parsley and serve hot, with extra sweet chili sauce.

SERVES 4

2 tbsp sunflower oil
1 lb/450 g pork tenderloin, cut into thin slices
2 tbsp sweet chili sauce, plus extra to serve
1 onion, sliced
2 carrots, cut into thin sticks
6 oz/175 g zucchini, cut into sticks
1 cup canned bamboo shoots, drained
4¾ cups cooked long-grain white rice
1 egg, beaten
1 tbsp chopped fresh parsley

NUTRITION

Calories 140; Sugars 3 g; Protein 3 g; Carbohydrate 20 g; Fat 17 g; Saturates 1 g

⭐⭐⭐   moderate
🕐   15 mins
🕐   20 mins

👨‍🍳 COOK'S TIP

For a really quick dish, add frozen mixed vegetables to the rice instead of the freshly prepared ones.

This is a very quick rice dish as it uses pre-cooked rice. It is therefore ideal when time is short or for a speedy lunchtime dish.

Stir-Fried Rice *with* Sausage

SERVES 4

2 tbsp sunflower oil
12 oz/350 g Chinese sausage, sliced thinly
2 tbsp soy sauce
1 onion, sliced
2 carrots, cut into thin sticks
1¾ cups frozen peas
¾ cup canned pineapple cubes, drained
4¾ cups cooked long-grain white rice
1 egg, beaten
1 tbsp chopped fresh parsley

1 Heat the sunflower oil in a preheated wok or large, heavy-based skillet. Add the sausage to the wok and cook for 5 minutes.

2 Stir in the soy sauce and allow to bubble for about 2–3 minutes, or until it becomes syrupy.

3 Add the onion, carrots, peas, and pineapple to the wok and cook for another 3 minutes.

4 Add the cooked rice to the wok and cook the mixture for about 2–3 minutes, or until the rice is completely heated through.

5 Drizzle the beaten egg over the top of the rice and cook, tossing the ingredients in the wok, until the egg sets.

6 Transfer the stir-fried rice to a large, warm serving bowl and scatter with the fresh parsley. Serve immediately.

NUTRITION
Calories *383*; Sugars *9 g*; Protein *19 g*;
Carbohydrate *42 g*; Fat *17 g*; Saturates *4 g*

moderate

5 mins

20 mins

COOK'S TIP

Cook extra rice and freeze it for later use in other rice dishes included in this book. Be sure to cool any leftover cooked rice quickly before freezing to avoid any risk of food poisoning, then reheat thoroughly.

Risotto is a creamy Italian dish made with risotto rice. This Chinese version is simply delicious!

Chinese Risotto

1 Heat the peanut oil in a preheated wok or large, heavy-based skillet.

2 Add the onion, garlic, and Chinese five-spice powder to the wok and cook for 1 minute.

3 Add the Chinese sausage, carrots, green bell pepper, and risotto rice to the wok and cook for 1 minute.

4 Gradually add the vegetable bouillon, a little at a time, stirring constantly until the liquid has been completely absorbed and the rice grains are tender.

5 Stir the chives into the wok with the last of the bouillon.

6 Transfer the Chinese risotto to warm serving bowls and serve immediately.

SERVES 4

2 tbsp peanut oil
1 onion, sliced
2 garlic cloves, crushed
1 tsp ground Chinese five-spice
8 oz/225 g Chinese sausage, sliced
3 small carrots, diced
1 green bell pepper, seeded and diced
1⅓ cups risotto rice
3½ cups vegetable or chicken bouillon
1 tbsp snipped fresh chives

NUTRITION

Calories *436*; Sugars *7 g*; Protein *13 g*; Carbohydrate *70 g*; Fat *14 g*; Saturates *4 g*

⭐⭐ easy
🕐 5 mins
🕐 30 mins

👨‍🍳 COOK'S TIP

Chinese sausage is highly flavored and is made from chopped pork fat, pork meat, and spices. Use a spicy Portuguese sausage if the Chinese sausage is unavailable.

This is a version of a favorite Thai dish, "mee krob," one of those exciting dishes which can vary from one day to the next.

Crispy Rice Noodles

SERVES 4

vegetable oil for deep-frying, plus an extra 1½ tbsp
7 oz/200 g dried rice vermicelli noodles
1 onion, chopped finely
4 garlic cloves, chopped finely
1 skinless, boneless chicken breast, chopped finely
2 fresh red bird's-eye chiles, seeded and sliced
4 tbsp dried Chinese black mushrooms, soaked, drained, and sliced thinly
3 tbsp dried shrimp
4 scallions, sliced
3 tbsp lime juice
2 tbsp each of soy sauce and fish sauce
2 tbsp rice wine vinegar
2 tbsp soft light brown sugar
2 eggs, beaten
3 tbsp chopped fresh cilantro
scallion curls, to garnish

1 Heat the oil for deep-frying in a preheated wok or large, heavy-based skillet until very hot. Deep-fry the noodles quickly, occasionally turning them, until puffed up, crisp and pale golden brown. Lift on to paper towels using a slotted spoon and drain well. Discard the oil.

2 Heat 1 tablespoon of the remaining oil and cook the onion and garlic for 1 minute. Add the chicken and cook for 3 minutes. Add the chiles, mushrooms, dried shrimp, and scallions.

3 Mix together the lime juice, soy sauce, fish sauce, rice wine vinegar, and sugar, then stir the mixture into the pan and cook for another minute. Remove the pan from the heat.

4 Heat the remaining oil in a skillet and pour in the eggs to coat the bottom of the pan evenly, making a thin omelet. Cook until set and golden, then turn it over and cook the other side. Turn out and roll up, then slice into long ribbon strips.

5 Toss together the fried noodles, stir-fried ingredients, cilantro, and omelet strips. Garnish with scallion curls and serve at once.

NUTRITION
Calories 490; Sugars 11 g; Protein 24 g;
Carbohydrate 63 g; Fat 16 g; Saturates 2 g

moderate

10 mins

15 mins

These noodles are highly spiced with chili and flavored with sesame seeds for a nutty taste, which is a true delight.

Spicy Japanese Noodles

1 Bring a large pan of water to a boil. Add the Japanese noodles to the pan and cook for 2–3 minutes. Drain the noodles thoroughly.

2 Toss the noodles with the sesame oil and sesame seeds.

3 Heat the sunflower oil in a preheated wok or large, heavy-based skillet.

4 Add the onion, snow peas, carrots, and cabbage to the wok and cook for about 5 minutes.

5 Add the sweet chili sauce to the wok and cook, stirring occasionally, for another 2 minutes.

6 Add the sesame noodles to the wok, toss well to combine and heat through for a further 2–3 minutes. (You may wish to serve the noodles separately, if so, transfer them to serving bowls.)

7 Transfer the mixture to warm serving bowls and garnish with the scallions. Serve immediately.

SERVES 4

1 lb 2 oz/450 g fresh Japanese noodles or dried thin egg noodles
1 tbsp sesame oil
1 tbsp sesame seeds
1 tbsp sunflower oil
1 red onion, sliced
$3\frac{1}{2}$ oz/100 g snow peas
2 carrots, sliced thinly
12 oz/350 g white cabbage, shredded
3 tbsp sweet chili sauce
2 scallions, sliced, to garnish

NUTRITION
Calories *381*; Sugars *12 g*; Protein *11 g*; Carbohydrate *59 g*; Fat *13 g*; Saturates *2 g*

✪✪✪   moderate

  5 mins

🕐 15 mins

🍳 COOK'S TIP

If fresh Japanese noodles are difficult to get hold of, use dried rice noodles or thin egg noodles, instead.

These rice noodles and vegetables are tossed in a crunchy peanut and chili sauce for a quick satay-flavored recipe.

Rice Noodles *with* Beans

SERVES 4

10 oz/275 g flat rice noodles
3 tbsp peanut oil
2 garlic cloves, crushed
2 shallots, sliced
8 oz/225 g fine green beans, sliced
3½ oz/100 g cherry tomatoes, halved
1 tsp dried chili flakes
4 tbsp crunchy peanut butter
⅔ cup coconut milk
1 tbsp tomato paste
sliced scallions, to garnish

1 Place the rice noodles in a large bowl and pour enough boiling water over to cover. Let stand for 10 minutes.

2 Heat the peanut oil in a preheated wok or large, heavy-based skillet.

3 Add the garlic and shallots and cook for 1 minute.

4 Drain the flat rice noodles thoroughly.

5 Add the green beans and drained noodles to the wok and cook for another 5 minutes.

6 Add the cherry tomatoes to the wok and mix well.

7 Mix together the chili flakes, peanut butter, coconut milk, and tomato paste until well combined.

8 Pour the chili and coconut mixture over the noodles, toss well to combine and heat through.

9 Transfer to warm serving dishes and garnish with the scallions. Serve immediately.

NUTRITION

Calories *259*; Sugars *9 g*; Protein *28 g*;
Carbohydrate *20 g*; Fat *8 g*; Saturates 1g

easy
5 mins
10 mins

🍳 COOK'S TIP

Add slices of chicken or beef to the recipe and stir-fry with the beans and noodles in step 4 for a more substantial main meal.

This simple, fast-food dish is sold from street food stalls in Thailand, with many varied additions of meat and vegetables.

Hot *and* Sour Noodles

1 Cook the noodles in a large pan of boiling water for 3–4 minutes, or according to the package directions. Drain well, return to the pan, toss with the sesame oil and set aside.

2 Heat the chili oil in a preheated wok or large, heavy-based skillet and quickly cook the garlic, onions, and white mushrooms until softened.

3 Add the black mushrooms, lime juice, soy sauce, and sugar and bring to a boil. Add the noodles and toss to mix.

4 Serve spooned over the Napa cabbage, garnished with cilantro and peanuts.

SERVES 4

9 oz/250 g dried medium egg noodles
1 tbsp sesame oil
1 tbsp chili oil
1 garlic clove, crushed
2 scallions, chopped finely
2 oz/55 g white mushrooms, sliced
1 cup dried Chinese black mushrooms, soaked, drained, and sliced
2 tbsp lime juice
3 tbsp light soy sauce
1 tsp sugar
shredded Napa cabbage, to serve

to garnish
2 tbsp shredded fresh cilantro
2 tbsp toasted peanuts, chopped

NUTRITION
Calories *140*; Sugars *3 g*; Protein *3 g*;
Carbohydrate *20 g*; Fat *17 g*; Saturates *1 g*

✪✪✪   moderate
           15 mins
           20 mins

🍳 COOK'S TIP

Thai chili oil is very hot, so if you want a milder flavor, use vegetable oil for the initial cooking instead, then add a final dribble of chili oil to season.

In this recipe, noodles are first boiled and then deep-fried for a crispy texture, and then served with stir-fried vegetables.

Fried Vegetable Noodles

SERVES 4

12 oz/350 g dried thin egg noodles
2 tbsp peanut oil
2 garlic cloves, crushed
½ tsp ground star anise
1 carrot, cut into very thin sticks
1 green bell pepper, seeded and cut into very thin sticks
1 onion, quartered and sliced
4½ oz/125 g broccoli florets
2¾ oz/75 g canned bamboo shoots
1 celery stalk, sliced
1 tbsp light soy sauce
⅔ cup vegetable bouillon
oil, for deep-frying
1 tsp cornstarch
2 tsp water

NUTRITION
Calories 229; Sugars 4 g; Protein 5 g;
Carbohydrate 20 g; Fat 15 g; Saturates 2 g

✪✪✪   moderate
🕐   5 mins
🕐   25 mins

1 Cook the noodles in a pan of boiling water for 1–2 minutes. Drain well and rinse under cold running water. Let the noodles drain thoroughly in a strainer until they are required.

2 Heat the peanut oil in a preheated wok or large, heavy-based skillet until smoking. Reduce the heat, add the garlic and star anise and cook for 30 seconds. Add the remaining vegetables and cook for 1–2 minutes.

3 Add the soy sauce and vegetable bouillon to the wok and cook over a low heat for 5 minutes.

4 Heat the oil for deep-frying in a separate wok or pan to 350°F/180°C, or until a cube of bread browns in 30 seconds.

5 Using a fork, twist the drained noodles and form them into rounds. Deep-fry them in batches until crisp, turning once. Let drain on paper towels.

6 Blend the cornstarch with the water to form a paste and stir into the vegetables. Bring to a boil, stirring until the sauce has thickened and cleared.

7 Arrange the noodles on warm serving plates, spoon the vegetables on top and serve immediately.

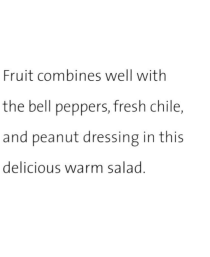

Fruit combines well with the bell peppers, fresh chile, and peanut dressing in this delicious warm salad.

Noodle *and* Mango Salad

1 Place the egg noodles in a large dish or bowl. Pour enough boiling water over to cover the noodles and let stand for 10 minutes.

2 Heat the peanut oil in a preheated wok or large, heavy-based skillet.

3 Add the shallots, garlic, chile, red, and green bell peppers to the wok and cook for 2–3 minutes.

4 Drain the egg noodles thoroughly in a strainer. Add the drained noodles and mango slices to the wok and heat through for about 2 minutes.

5 Transfer the noodle and mango salad to warmed serving dishes and scatter with chopped peanuts.

6 To make the dressing, mix together the peanut butter, coconut milk, and tomato paste, then spoon it over the noodle salad. Serve immediately.

SERVES 4

9 oz/250 g dried medium egg noodles
2 tbsp peanut oil
4 shallots, sliced
2 garlic cloves, crushed
1 fresh red chile, seeded and sliced
1 red bell pepper, seeded and sliced
1 green bell pepper, seeded and sliced
1 ripe mango, peeled, pitted and sliced into thin strips
¼ cup salted peanuts, chopped

dressing
4 tbsp peanut butter
generous ⅓ cup coconut milk
1 tbsp tomato paste

NUTRITION
Calories *368*; Sugars *11 g*; Protein *11 g*; Carbohydrate *24 g*; Fat *26 g*; Saturates *5 g*

⊛⊛   easy
◔   15 mins
◷   15 mins

🍳 COOK'S TIP

If preferred, gently heat the peanut dressing before pouring it over the warm noodle salad.

Cellophane or thread noodles can be easily re-heated, unlike other noodles, which must be served as soon as they are cooked.

Yellow Bean Noodles

SERVES 4

6 oz/175 g cellophane noodles
1 tbsp peanut oil
1 leek, sliced
2 garlic cloves, crushed
1 lb/450 g ground chicken
scant 2 cups chicken bouillon
1 tsp chili sauce
2 tbsp yellow bean sauce
4 tbsp light soy sauce
1 tsp sesame oil
snipped fresh chives, to garnish

1 Place the cellophane noodles in a bowl, pour enough boiling water over to cover and soak for 15 minutes.

2 Drain the noodles thoroughly and cut into short lengths with a pair of kitchen scissors.

3 Heat the oil in a preheated wok or large, heavy-based skillet and stir-fry the leek and garlic for 30 seconds.

4 Add the chicken to the wok and cook for 4–5 minutes, until completely cooked through.

5 Add the chicken bouillon, chili sauce, yellow bean sauce, and soy sauce to the wok and cook for 3–4 minutes.

6 Add the drained noodles and sesame oil to the wok and cook, tossing to mix well, for 4–5 minutes.

7 Spoon the mixture into warm serving bowls, sprinkle with snipped chives and serve immediately.

NUTRITION
Calories 212; Sugars 0.5 g; Protein 28 g;
Carbohydrate 10 g; Fat 7 g; Saturates 2 g

easy

5 mins

30 mins

COOK'S TIP

Cellophane noodles are readily available from many food stores and Chinese supermarkets.

Fish and fruit are tossed with a trio of bell peppers in this spicy dish, which can be served with noodles for a quick, healthy meal.

Noodles *with* Cod *and* Mango

1 Place the egg noodles in a large bowl and pour over enough boiling water to cover. Let stand for about 10 minutes.

2 Place the cod in a large bowl. Add the paprika and toss well to coat the fish.

3 Heat the sunflower oil in a preheated wok or large, heavy-based skillet.

4 Add the onion, orange, red, and green bell peppers, and baby corn cobs to the wok and cook for about 5 minutes.

5 Add the cod to the wok with the mango and cook for a further 2–3 minutes, or until the fish is tender.

6 Add the beansprouts to the wok and toss well to combine.

7 Mix together the tomato catsup, soy sauce, sherry, and cornstarch. Add the mixture to the wok and cook, stirring occasionally, until the juices thicken.

8 Drain the noodles thoroughly and transfer to warm serving bowls. Transfer the cod and mango stir-fry to separate serving bowls.

SERVES 4

9 oz/250 g dried egg noodles
1 lb/450 g skinless cod fillet, cut into thin strips
1 tbsp paprika
2 tbsp sunflower oil
1 red onion, sliced
1 orange bell pepper, seeded and sliced
1 red bell pepper, seeded and sliced
1 green bell pepper, seeded and sliced
3 1/2 oz/100 g baby corn cobs, halved lengthwise
1 mango, peeled, pitted and sliced
1 cup beansprouts
2 tbsp tomato catsup
2 tbsp soy sauce
2 tbsp medium sherry
1 tsp cornstarch

NUTRITION
Calories *274*; Sugars *11 g*; Protein *25 g*; Carbohydrate *26 g*; Fat *8 g*; Saturates *1 g*

✪✪✪   moderate
        10 mins
        25 mins

This dish combines meat, vegetables, shrimp, and noodles in a curried coconut sauce. Serve as an entrée or as an accompaniment.

Special Noodles

SERVES 4

9 oz/250 g dried thin rice noodles
4 tbsp peanut oil
2 garlic cloves, crushed
2 fresh red chiles, seeded and very
   finely chopped
1 tsp grated fresh gingerroot
2 tbsp Madras curry paste
2 tbsp rice wine vinegar
1 tbsp superfine sugar
8 oz/225 g cooked ham, shredded finely
$3\frac{1}{2}$ oz/100 g canned water chestnuts,
   drained and sliced
$3\frac{1}{2}$ oz/100 g mushrooms, sliced
$\frac{3}{4}$ cup frozen peas
1 red bell pepper, seeded and sliced thinly
$3\frac{1}{2}$ oz/100 g peeled, cooked shrimp
2 large eggs
4 tbsp coconut milk
$\frac{1}{4}$ cup shredded coconut
2 tbsp chopped fresh cilantro

NUTRITION
Calories *409*; Sugars *12 g*; Protein *24 g*;
Carbohydrate *28 g*; Fat *23 g*; Saturates *8 g*

✪✪✪   moderate
🕐   5 mins
🕐   25 mins

1 Place the rice noodles in a large bowl, pour enough boiling water over to cover and let soak for about 10 minutes. Drain the noodles thoroughly, then toss with 2 tablespoons of peanut oil.

2 Heat the remaining peanut oil in a preheated wok or large, heavy-based skillet until really hot.

3 Add the garlic, chiles, ginger, curry paste, rice wine vinegar, and superfine sugar to the wok and cook for 1 minute.

4 Add the ham, water chestnuts, mushrooms, peas, and red bell pepper to the wok and cook for 5 minutes.

5 Add the noodles and shrimp to the wok and cook for 2 minutes.

6 In a small bowl, beat together the eggs and coconut milk. Drizzle the mixture into the wok and cook until the egg sets.

7 Add the coconut and fresh cilantro to the wok and toss to combine. Transfer the noodles to warm serving dishes and serve immediately.

These noodles make a meal in themselves, although if served as an accompaniment, they are ideal with plain vegetable or fish dishes.

Curried Shrimp Noodles

1 Cook the noodles in a pan of boiling water for 3–4 minutes. Drain the noodles well, rinse under cold running water and drain again.

2 Heat 2 tablespoons of the oil in a wok. Add the onion and ham and cook for 1 minute. Add the curry powder and cook for a further 30 seconds.

3 Stir the noodles and fish bouillon into the wok and cook for 2–3 minutes. Remove the noodles from the wok and keep warm.

4 Heat the remaining oil in the wok. Add the shrimp, garlic, and scallions and cook for about 1 minute.

5 Stir in the remaining ingredients. Pour the mixture over the noodles, toss to mix and garnish with fresh chives, to serve.

SERVES 4

8 oz/225 g dried egg noodles
4 tbsp vegetable oil
1 onion, sliced
2 ham slices, shredded
2 tbsp Chinese curry powder
²⁄₃ cup fish bouillon
8 oz/225 g peeled, raw shrimp
2 garlic cloves, crushed
6 scallions, chopped
1 tbsp light soy sauce
2 tbsp Peking sauce
1 tbsp dry sherry
2 tsp lime juice
snipped chives, to garnish

NUTRITION
Calories *246*; Sugars *1 g*; Protein *17 g*;
Carbohydrate *14 g*; Fat *14 g*; Saturates *2 g*

⊛⊛   easy

◔   5 mins

🕐   15 mins

🍳 **COOK'S TIP**

Peking sauce is made from soybeans, sugar, flour, vinegar, salt, garlic, chile, and sesame oil. Sold in cans or jars, it will keep in the refrigerator for several months once opened if kept in a sealed container.

Delicately scented with sesame, lime, and cilantro, these noodles make an unusual lunch or supper dish.

Sesame Noodles *with* Shrimp

SERVES 4

1 garlic clove, chopped
1 scallion, chopped
1 small fresh red chile, seeded and sliced
1 tsp chopped fresh cilantro
10½ oz/300 g dried fine egg noodles
2 tbsp vegetable oil
2 tsp sesame oil
1 tsp shrimp paste
8 oz/225 g peeled, raw shrimp,
2 tbsp lime juice
2 tbsp fish sauce
1 tsp sesame seeds, toasted

1 Use a pestle and mortar to grind the garlic, onion, chile, and cilantro into a smooth paste.

2 Cook the noodles in a pan of boiling water for 4 minutes, or according to the package directions.

3 Meanwhile, heat the oils in a preheated wok or large, heavy-based skillet and stir in the shrimp paste and cilantro mixture. Stir over a medium heat for 1 minute.

4 Add the shrimp and cook for 2 minutes. Stir in the lime juice and fish sauce and cook for another 1 minute.

5 Drain the noodles and toss them into the wok. Sprinkle with the sesame seeds and serve.

NUTRITION
Calories *430*; Sugars *2 g*; Protein *23 g*;
Carbohydrate *56 g*; Fat *15 g*; Saturates *3 g*

easy

5 mins

10 mins

🍳 COOK'S TIP

The roots of cilantro are widely used in Thai cooking, so if you can buy fresh cilantro with the root attached, the whole plant can be used in this dish for maximum flavor. If not, just use the stems and leaves.

This is a special well-known dish, which is a delicious meal in itself, packed with chicken, shrimp, and vegetables.

Singapore Noodles

1 Place the noodles in a large bowl and pour enough water over to cover. Let stand for 4 minutes, or until soft. Drain well and set aside.

2 Heat 2 tablespoons of the oil in a preheated wok or large, heavy-based skillet. Add the eggs and stir until set. Remove the cooked eggs from the wok, set aside and keep warm.

3 Add the remaining oil to the wok. Add the garlic and chili powder and cook for 30 seconds.

4 Add the chicken and cook for 4–5 minutes, until just beginning to brown.

5 Stir in the celery, green bell pepper, scallions, water chestnuts, and chiles and cook for a further 8 minutes, or until the chicken is cooked through.

6 Add the shrimp and the drained noodles to the wok, together with the beansprouts, and toss to mix well.

7 Break the cooked egg with a fork and arrange it over the noodles, drizzle over the sesame oil and serve immediately.

SERVES 4

8 oz/225 g dried egg noodles
6 tbsp vegetable oil
4 eggs, beaten
3 garlic cloves, crushed
1½ tsp chili powder
8 oz/225 g skinless, boneless chicken, cut into thin strips
3 celery stalks, sliced
1 green bell pepper, seeded and sliced
4 scallions, sliced
1 oz/25 g water chestnuts, quartered
2 fresh red chiles, sliced
10 oz/300 g peeled, cooked shrimp
1¾ cups beansprouts
2 tsp sesame oil

NUTRITION
Calories 627; Sugars 3 g; Protein 44 g; Carbohydrate 44 g;Fat 32 g; Saturates 4 g

★★★ moderate

🕐 5 mins

🕐 20 mins

COOK'S TIP

When mixing pre-cooked ingredients into the dish, such as the egg and noodles, ensure that they are heated right through when ready to serve.

The combination of ingredients in this classic thai noodle dish varies, but it commonly contains a mixture of pork and shrimp or other seafood.

Pad Thai Noodles

SERVES 4

9 oz/250 g dried flat rice noodles
3 tbsp peanut oil
3 garlic cloves, chopped finely
4 1/2 oz/125 g pork tenderloin, chopped into
  1/4-inch/5-mm pieces
7 oz/200 g peeled, cooked shrimp
1 tbsp sugar
3 tbsp fish sauce
1 tbsp tomato catsup
1 tbsp lime juice
2 eggs, beaten
1 1/4 cups beansprouts

to garnish
1 tsp dried red chili flakes
2 scallions, sliced thickly
2 tbsp chopped fresh cilantro

1 Place the rice noodles in a large bowl and pour enough boiling water over to cover. Let stand for about 10 minutes, or according to the package directions. Drain well and set aside.

2 Heat the oil in a preheated wok or large, heavy-based skillet and cook the garlic over a high heat for 30 seconds. Add the pork and cook for 2–3 minutes, until browned.

3 Stir in the shrimp, then add the sugar, fish sauce, tomato catsup, and lime juice, and cook for another 30 seconds.

4 Stir in the eggs and cook until lightly set. Stir in the noodles, then add the beansprouts and cook for a further 30 seconds.

5 Turn out on to a warm serving dish and scatter with chili flakes, scallions, and cilantro.

NUTRITION

Calories *477*; Sugars *6 g*; Protein *26 g*;
Carbohydrate *60 g*; Fat *14 g*; Saturates *3 g*

easy

10 mins

15 mins

🍳 COOK'S TIP

Drain the rice noodles well before adding to the pan, as excess moisture will spoil the texture of the dish.

This dish is usually served as a snack or light meal. It may also be served as an accompaniment to plain meat and fish dishes.

Cantonese Fried Noodles

1 Cook the noodles in a pan of boiling water for 2–3 minutes. Drain well, rinse under cold running water and drain thoroughly again.

2 Heat 1 tablespoon of the oil in a preheated wok or skillet, swirling it around until it is really hot

3 Add the noodles and cook for 1–2 minutes. Drain the noodles and set aside until required.

4 Heat the remaining oil in the wok. Add the beef and cook for 2–3 minutes. Add the cabbage, bamboo shoots, scallions, and beans to the wok and cook for 1–2 minutes.

5 Add the soy sauce, beef bouillon, dry sherry, and light brown sugar to the wok, stirring to mix well.

6 Stir the noodles into the mixture in the wok, tossing to mix well. Transfer to serving bowls, garnish with chopped parsley and serve immediately.

SERVES 4

12 oz/350 g egg noodles
3 tbsp vegetable oil
1½ lb/675 g lean beef steak, cut into
    thin strips
4½ oz/125 g green cabbage, shredded
2¾ oz/75 g canned, drained bamboo shoots
6 scallions, sliced
1 oz/25 g fine green beans, halved
1 tbsp dark soy sauce
2 tbsp beef bouillon
1 tbsp dry sherry
1 tbsp light brown sugar
2 tbsp chopped fresh parsley, to garnish

NUTRITION
Calories 385; Sugars 6 g; Protein 38 g;
Carbohydrate 21 g; Fat 17 g; Saturates 4 g

easy

5 mins

15 mins

Index